DO YOU KNOW

Tigers?

Written by
Alain M. Bergeron
Michel Quintin
Sampar

Illustrations by
Sampar

Translated by
Solange Messier

Fitzhenry & Whiteside

First published as "Savais-Tu? Les tigres" by Editions Michel Quintin, Québec, Canada, J0E 2N0
Published in Canada by Fitzhenry & Whiteside, 195 Allstate Parkway, Markham, Ontario L3R 4T8
Published in the United States by Fitzhenry & Whiteside, 311 Washington Street, Brighton, Massachusetts 02135

www.fitzhenry.ca godwit@fitzhenry.ca

10 9 8 7 6 5 4 3 2 1

Library and Archives Canada Cataloguing in Publication
Do You Know Tigers?
ISBN 978-1-55455-355-6 (pbk.)
Data available on file

Publisher Cataloging-in-Publication Data (U.S.)
Do You Know Tigers?
ISBN 978-1-55455-355-6 (pbk.)
Data available on file

Fitzhenry & Whiteside acknowledges with thanks the Canada Council for the Arts, and the Ontario Arts Council for their support of our publishing program. We acknowledge the financial support of the Government of Canada through the Canada Book Fund (CBF) for our publishing activities.

**Canada Council
for the Arts**

**Conseil des Arts
du Canada**

ONTARIO ARTS COUNCIL
CONSEIL DES ARTS DE L'ONTARIO
an Ontario government agency
un organisme du gouvernement de l'Ontario

Cover and text design by Daniel Choi
Cover image by Sampar

Printed in China

MIX
Paper from
responsible sources
FSC® C016245

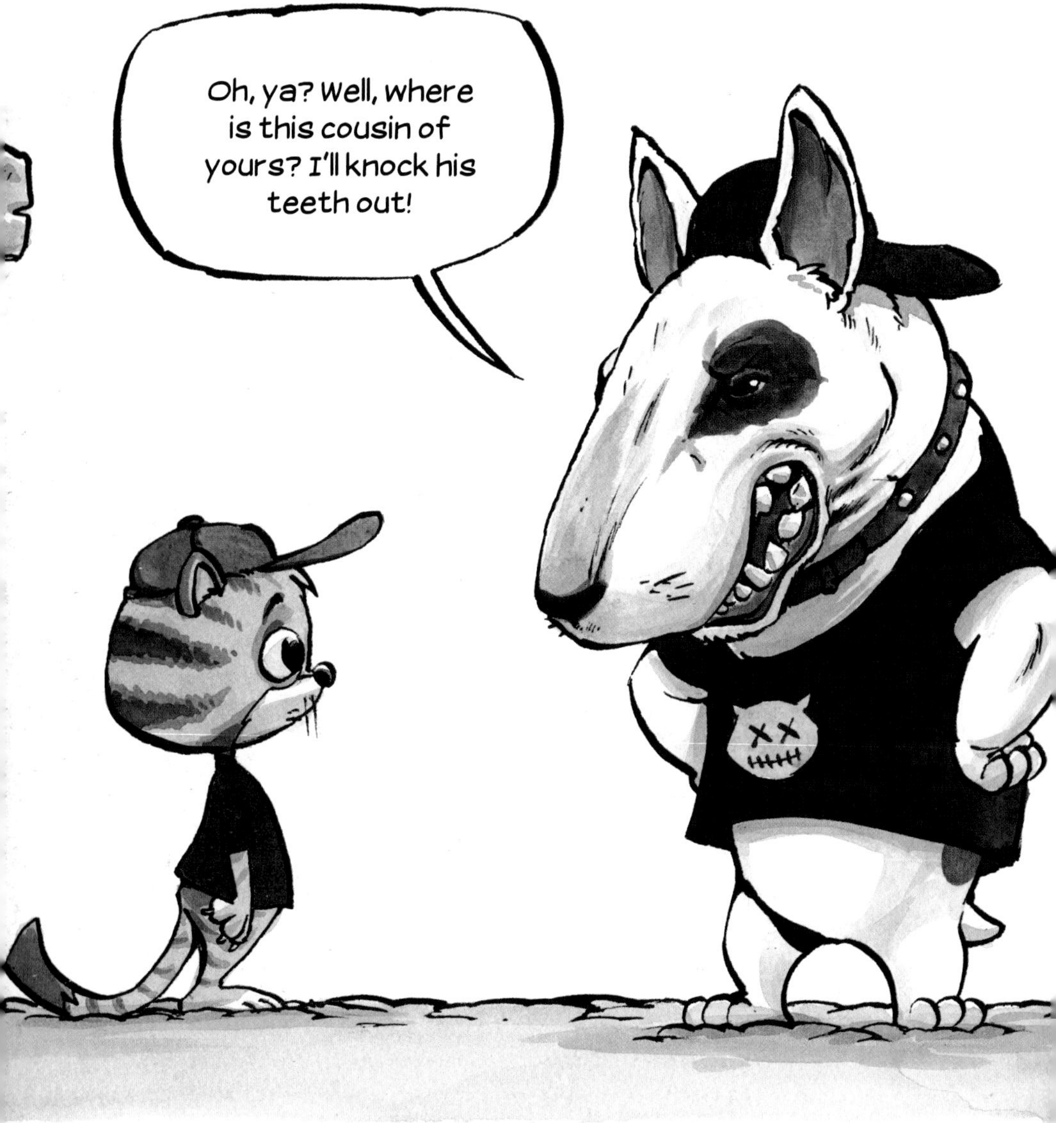
Oh, ya? Well, where is this cousin of yours? I'll knock his teeth out!

Tigers are the largest **species** of the **feline** family.

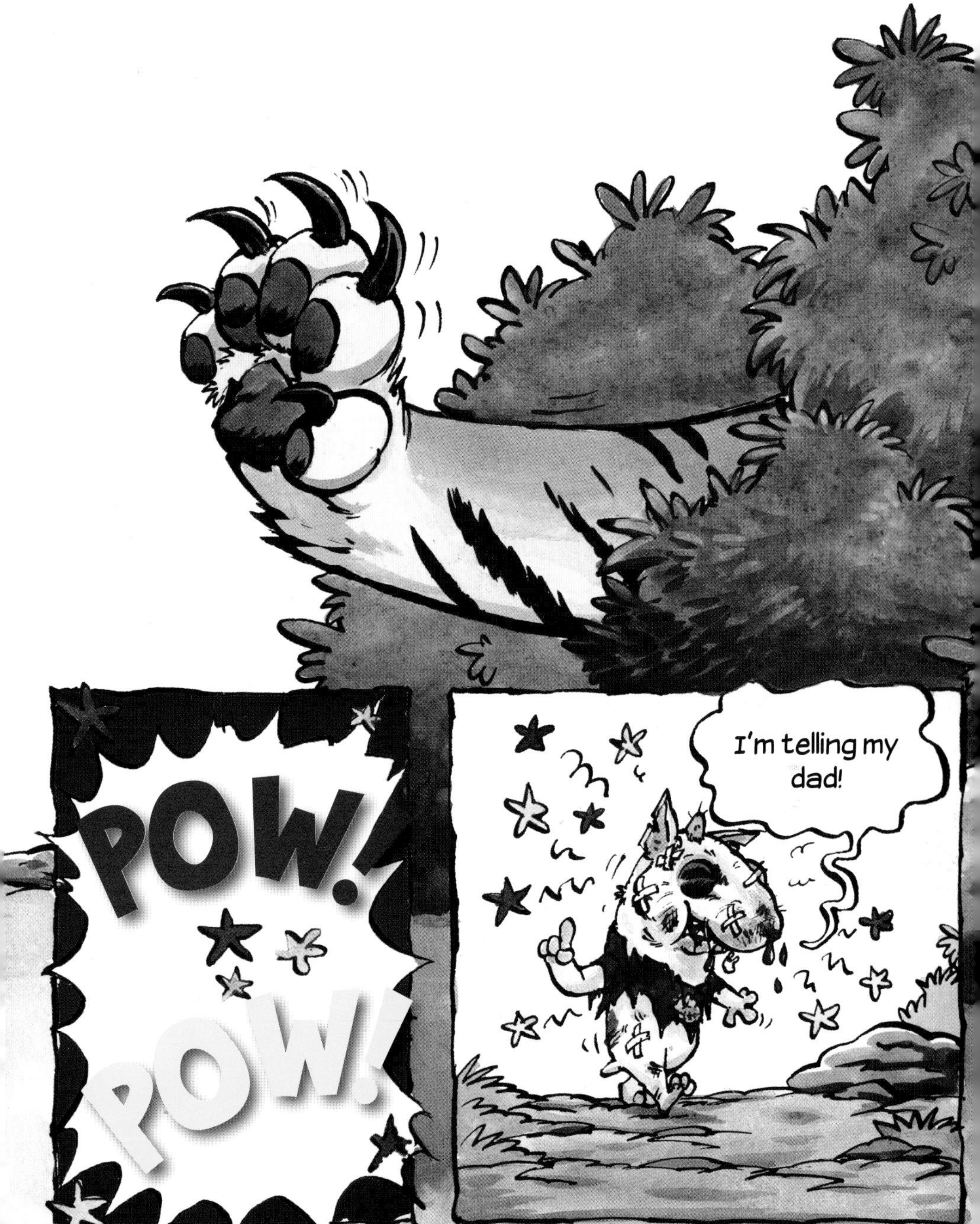
POW!
POW!
I'm telling my dad!

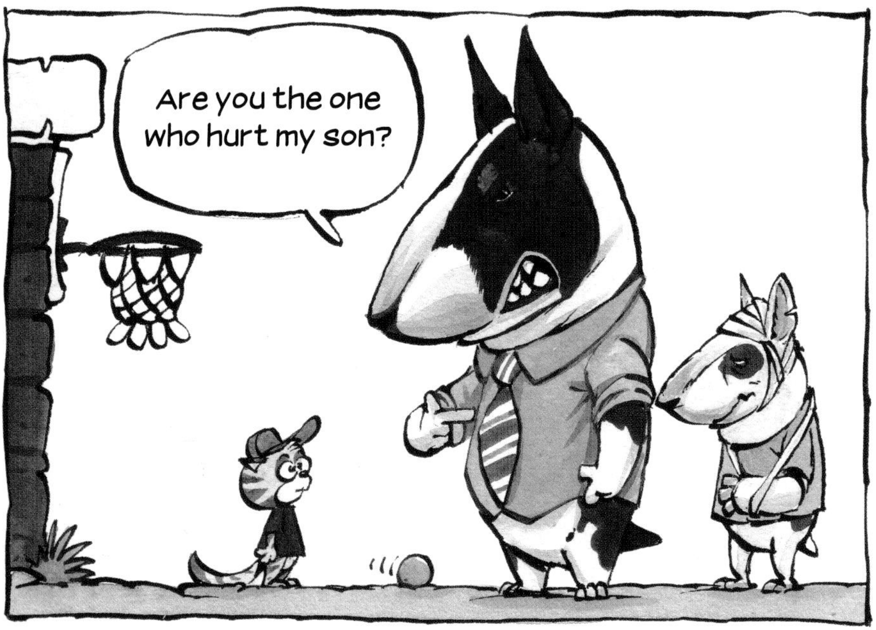
Are you the one who hurt my son?

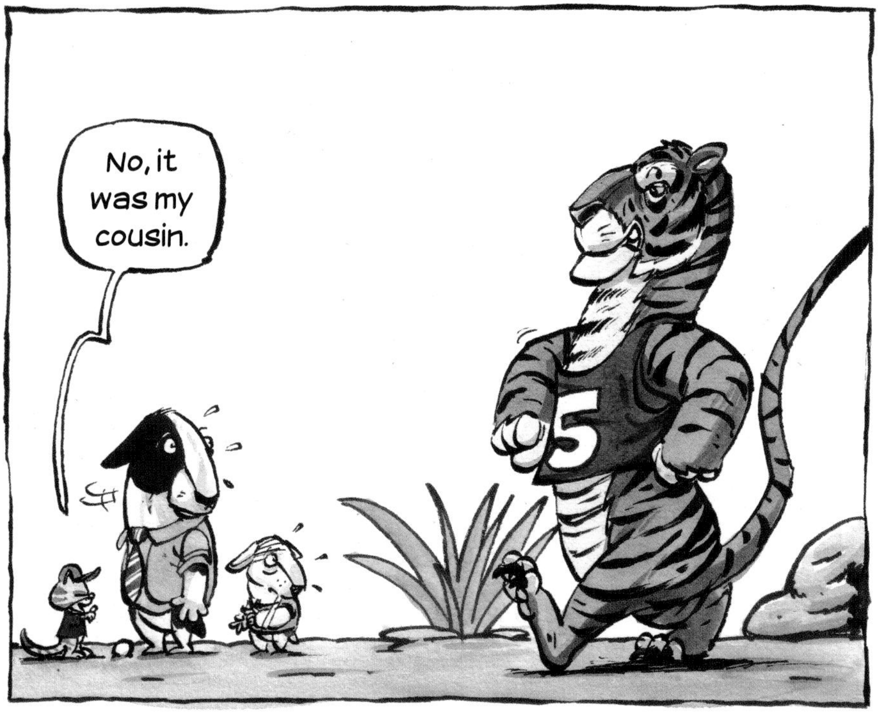
No, it was my cousin.

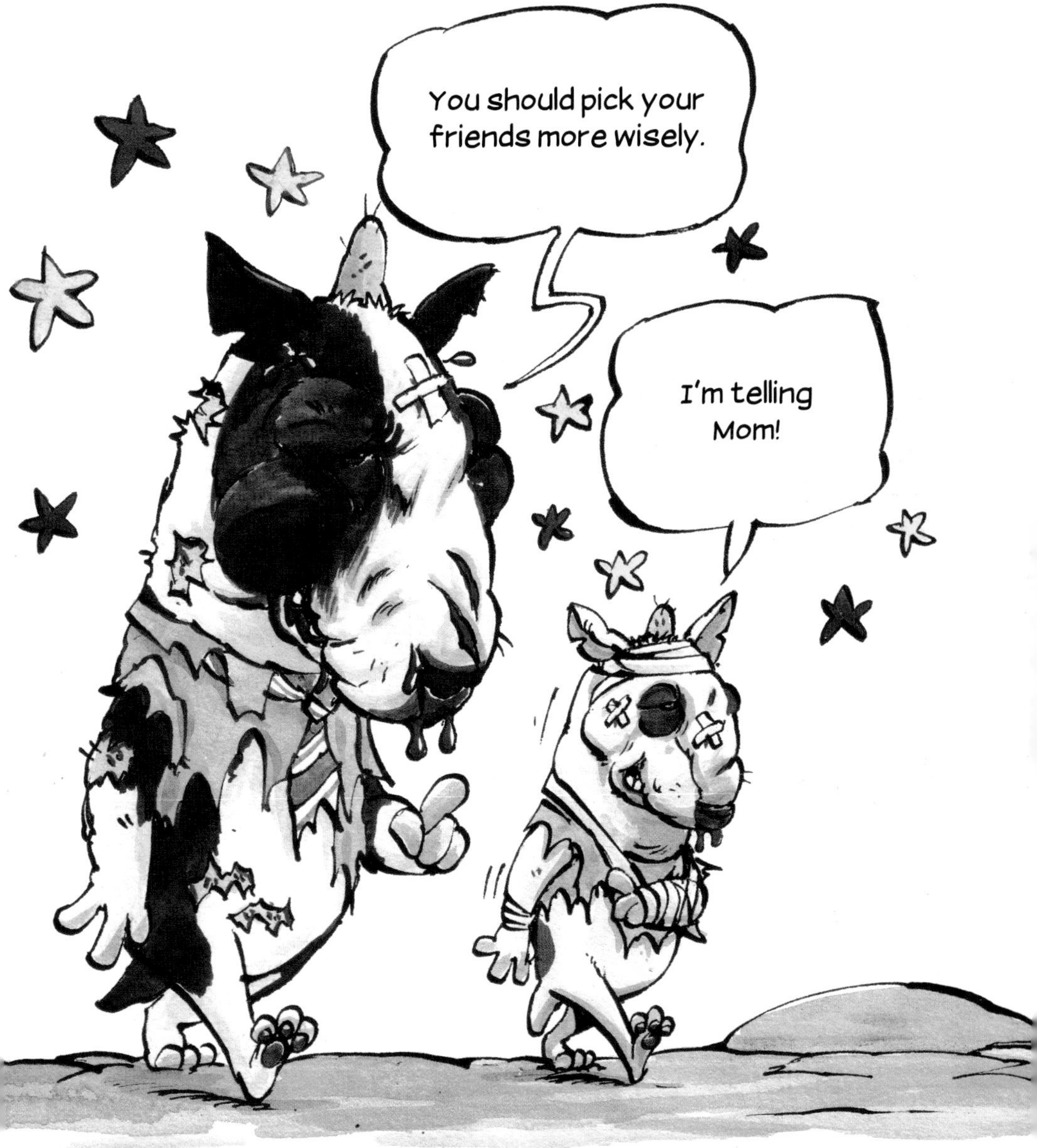
You should pick your friends more wisely.
I'm telling Mom!

Tigers can measure over 3 metres (10 feet) long, excluding their tails, and weigh up to 260 kilograms (573 pounds). A male Siberian tiger weighed a record 384 kilograms (846 pounds).

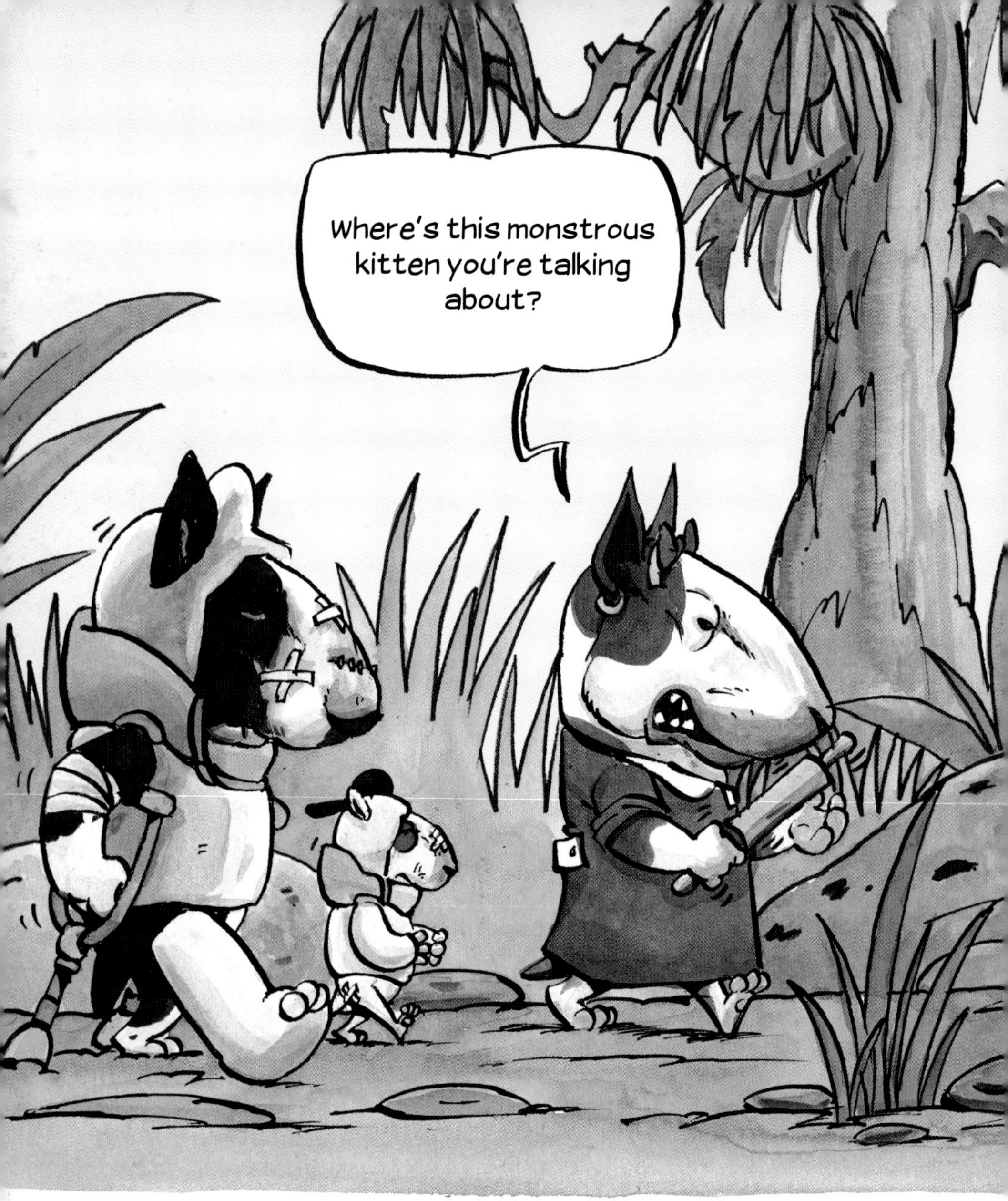
Where's this monstrous kitten you're talking about?

The black stripes on a tiger's orange fur help it blend into its surroundings.

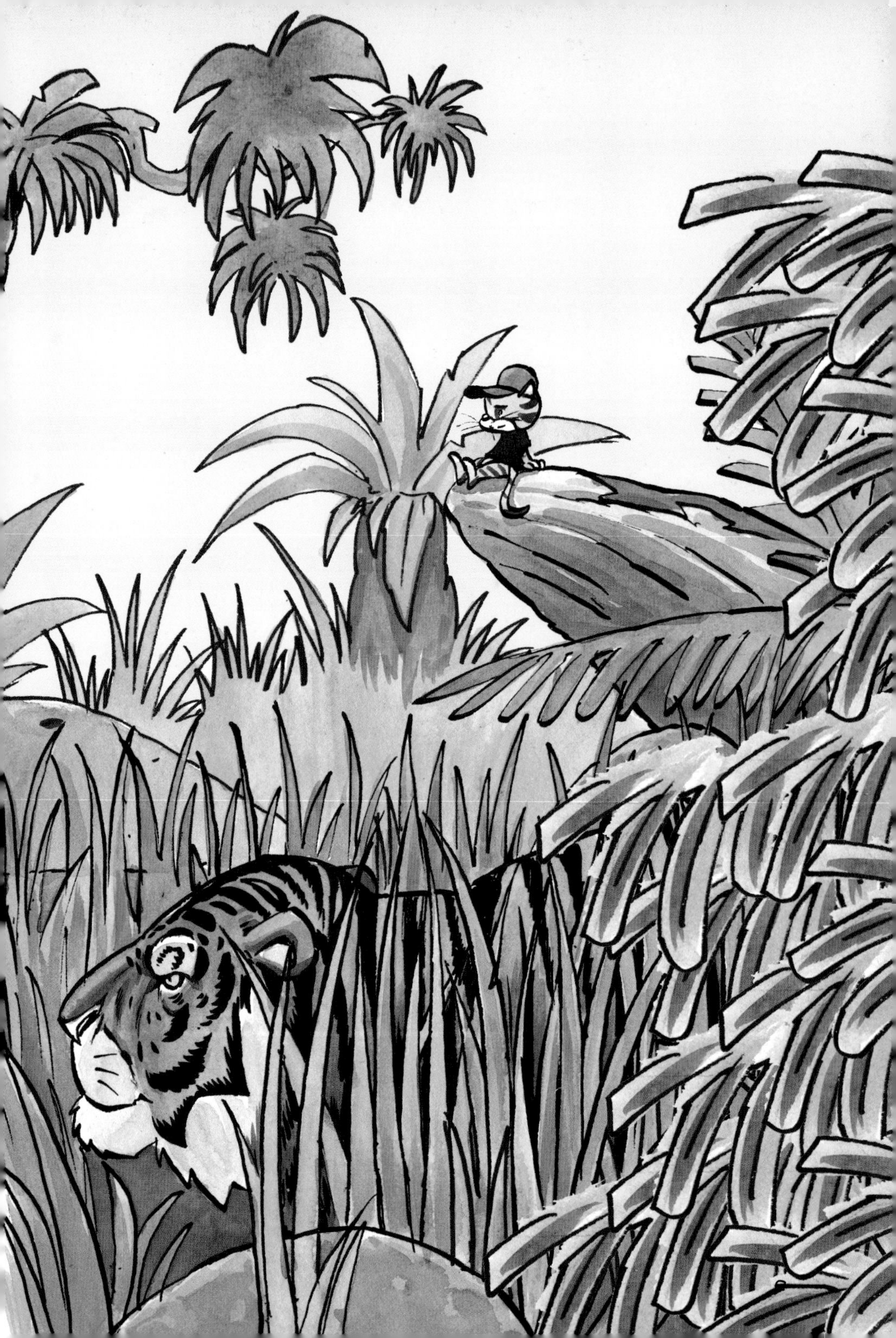

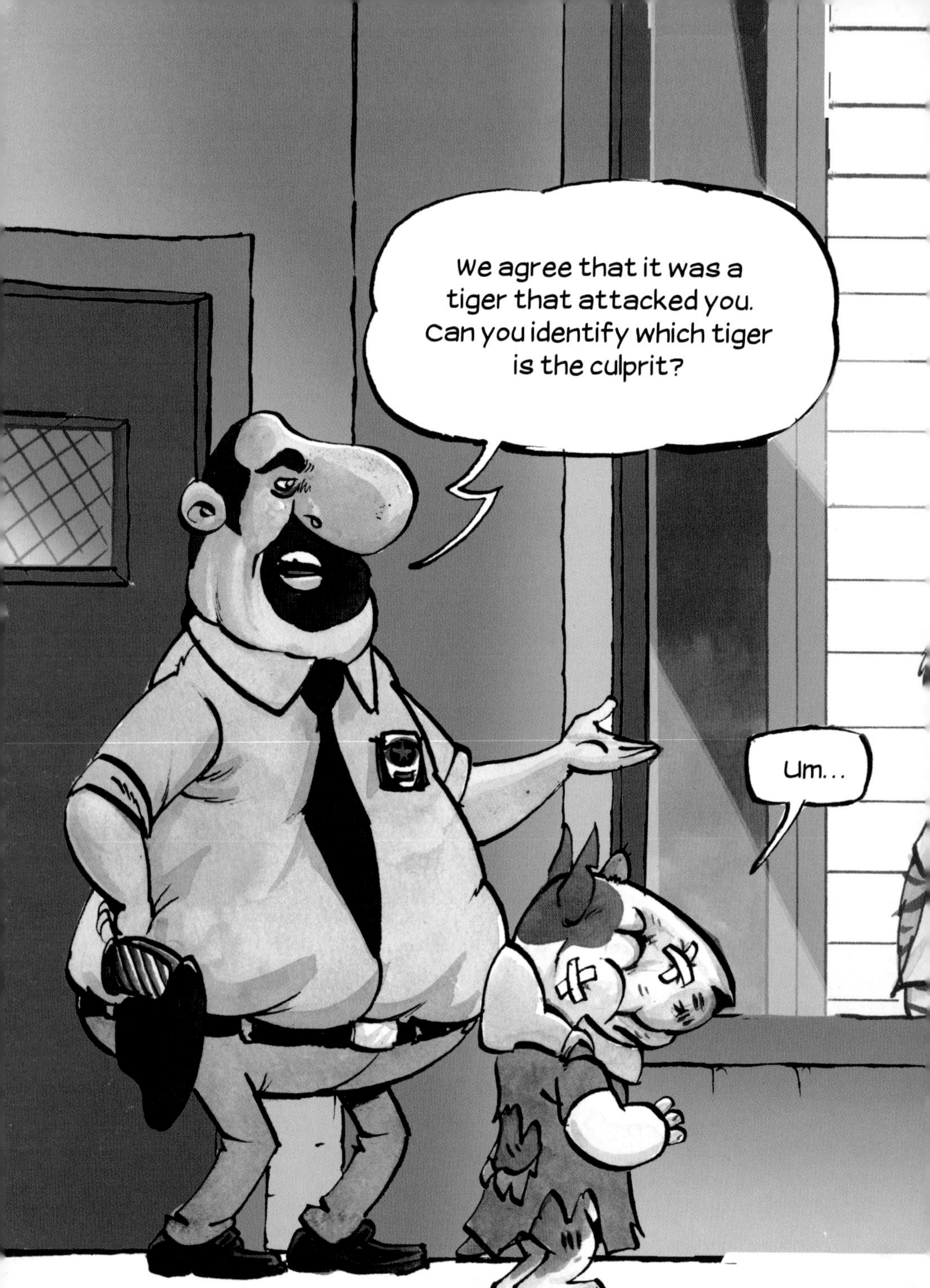
We agree that it was a tiger that attacked you. Can you identify which tiger is the culprit?
Um...

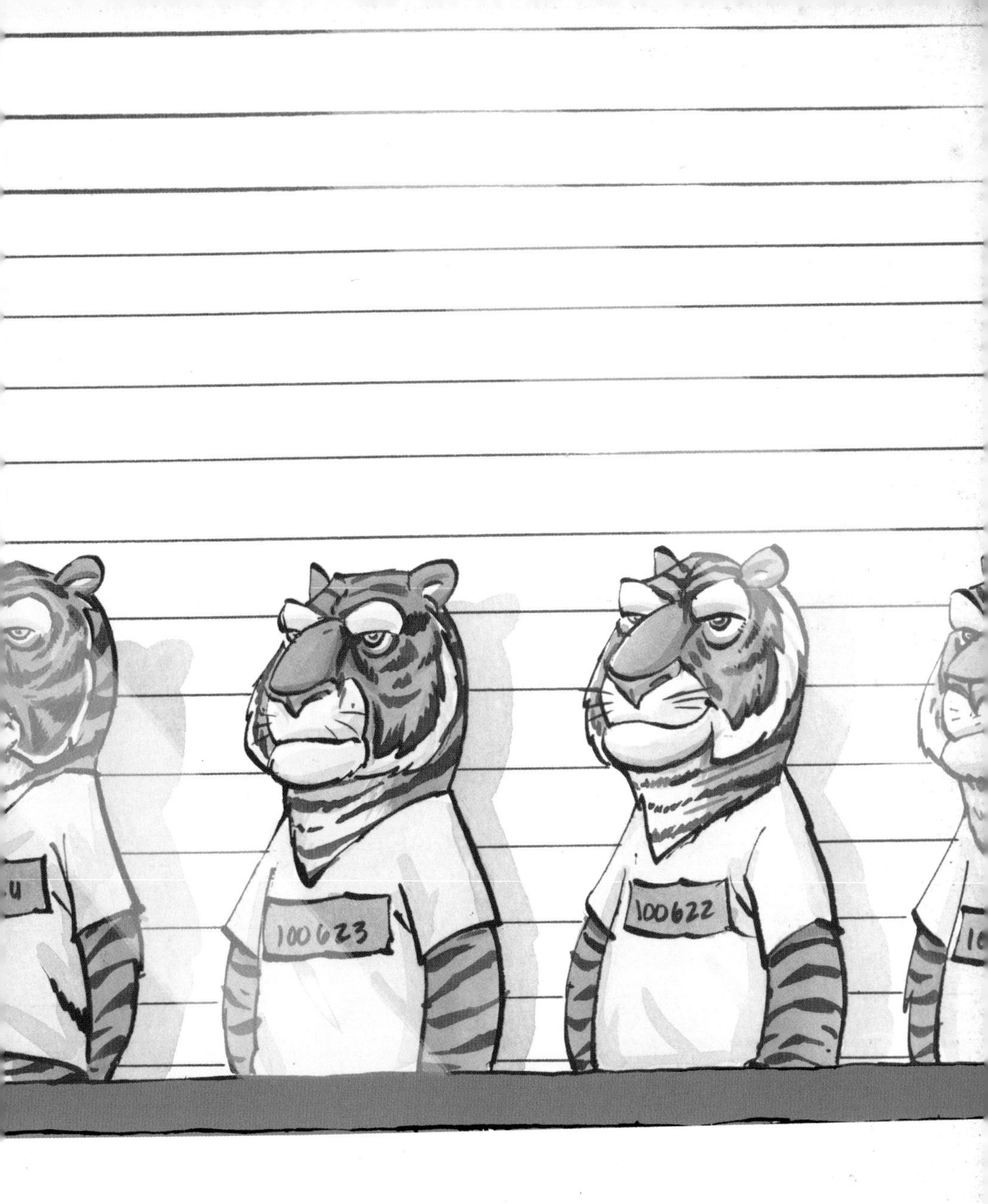
100623
100622

Just like every person's fingerprints are unique, so are the stripes on every tiger's head.

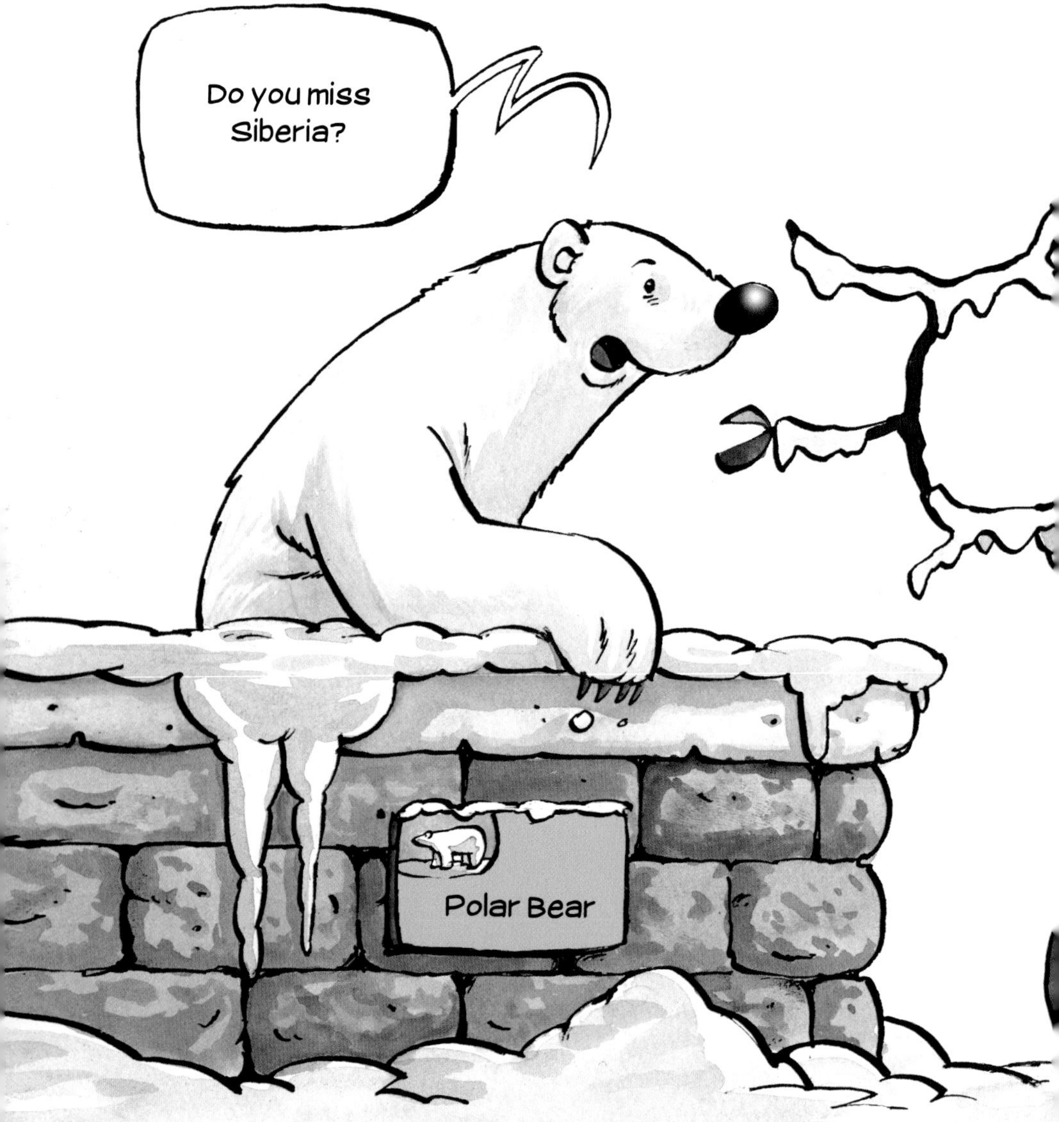
Do you miss Siberia?
Polar Bear

Certain groups and **subspecies** of tigers live in cold regions where the temperature can reach -43°C (-45°F).

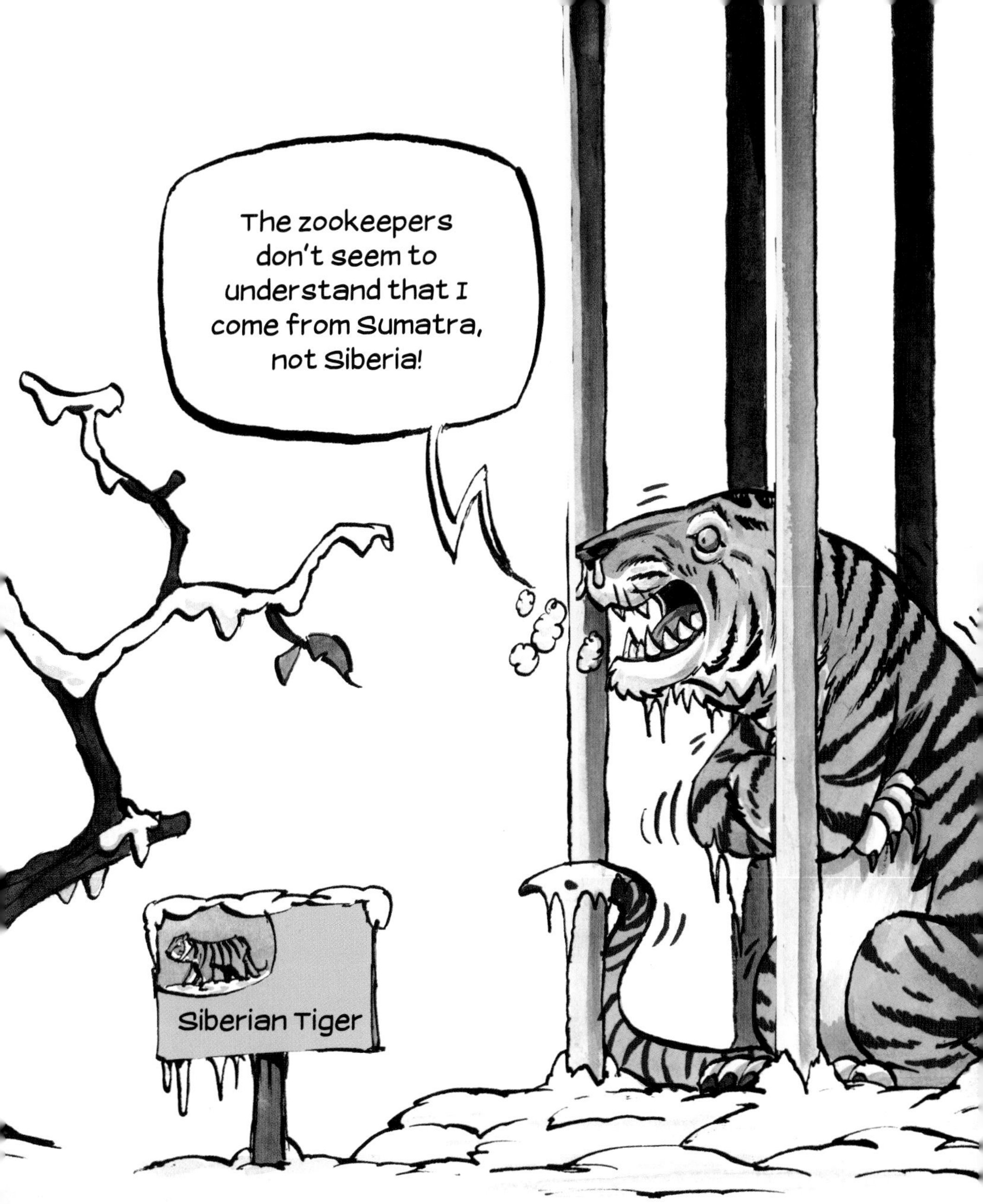
The zookeepers don't seem to understand that I come from Sumatra, not Siberia!
Siberian Tiger

Other tigers, however, live in extremely hot regions where the temperatures reach 43°C (109°F).

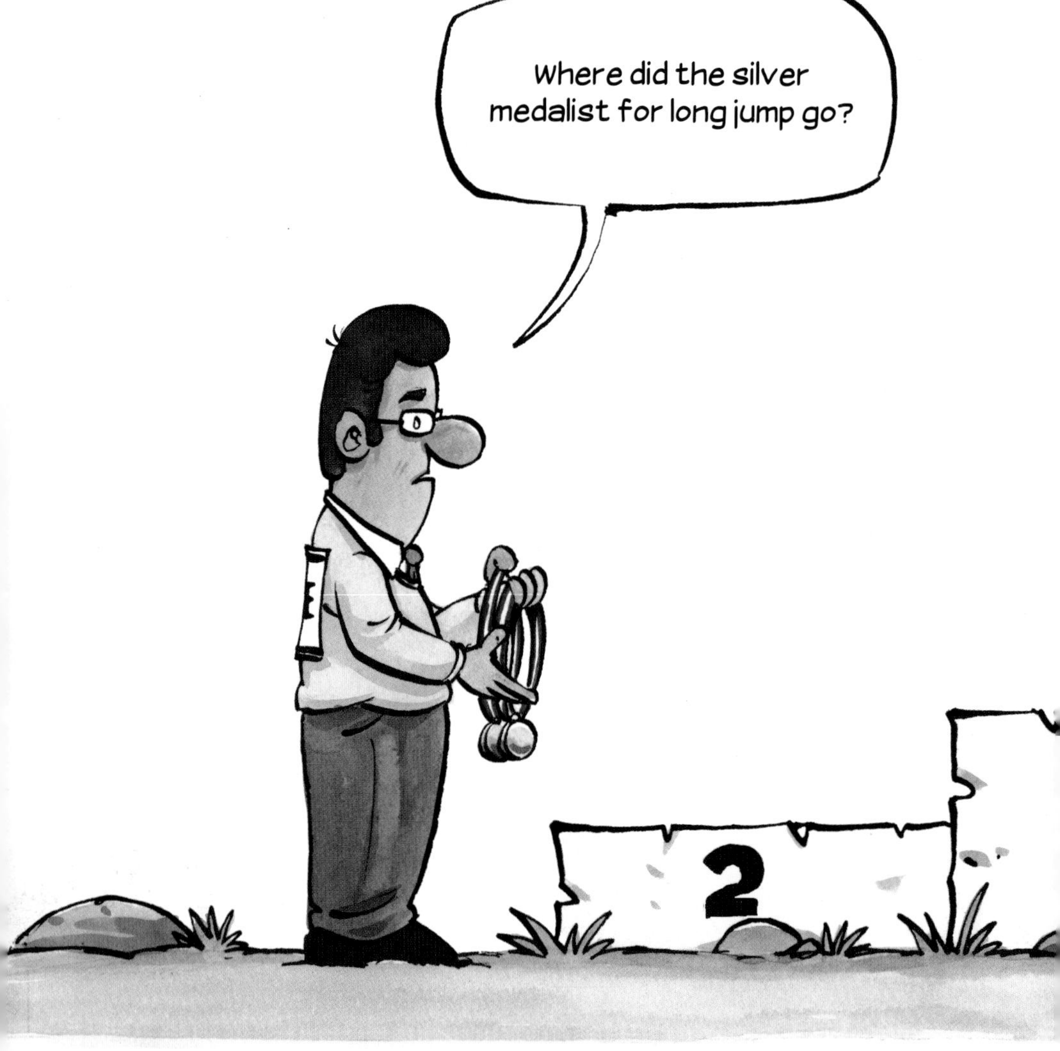
Where did the silver medalist for long jump go?
2

This **mammal** can jump up to 4 metres (13 feet) high and forward leap up to 10 metres (33 feet). In comparison, the Olympic records

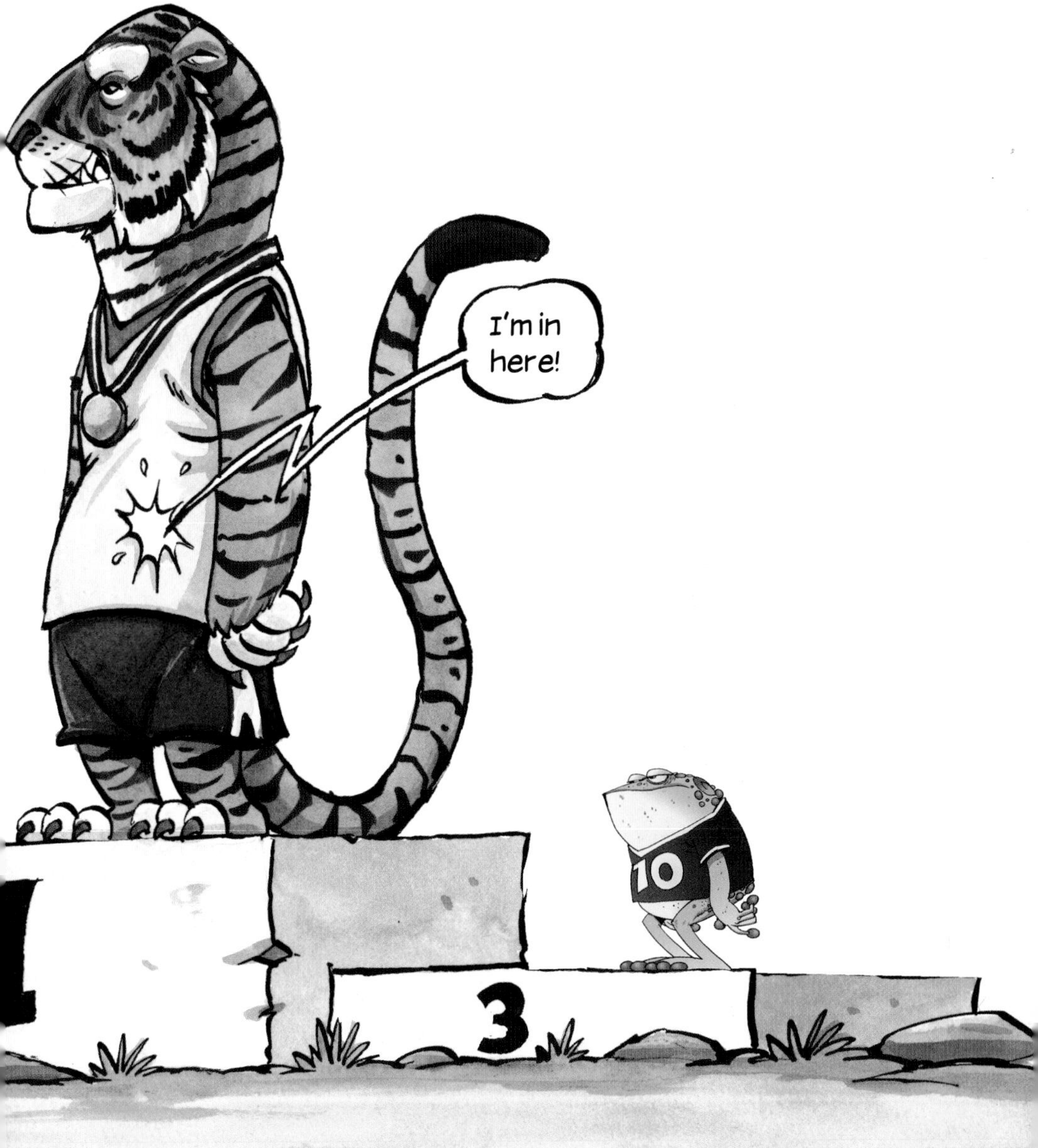
I'm in here!
10
3

for humans included a jump of 2.45 metres (8 feet) high and a forward leap of 8.95 metres (29.3 feet) long.

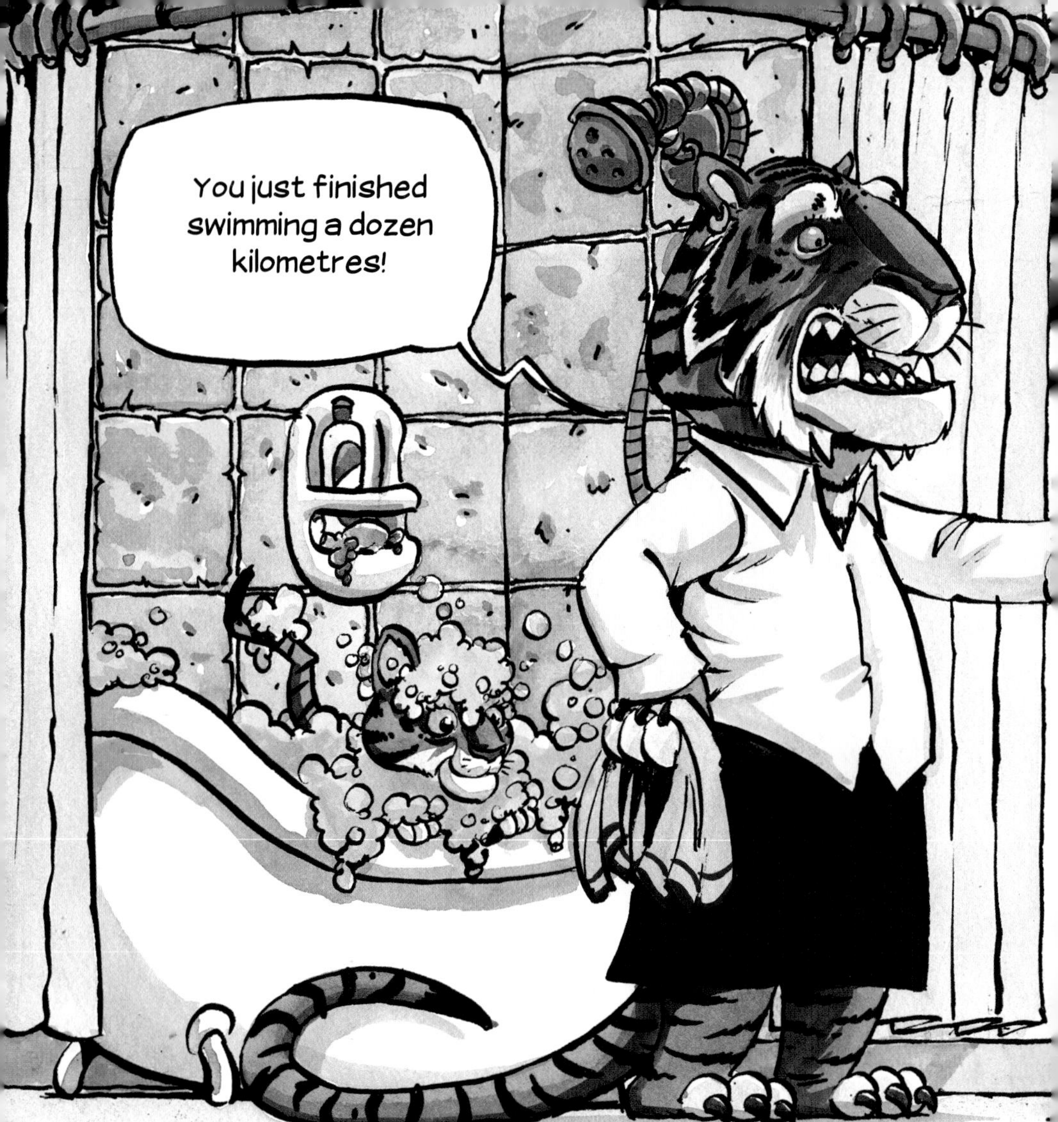
You just finished swimming a dozen kilometres!

Tigers love water and they are excellent swimmers. A Sumatran tiger holds the endurance record for swimming a distance of 29 kilometres (18 miles).

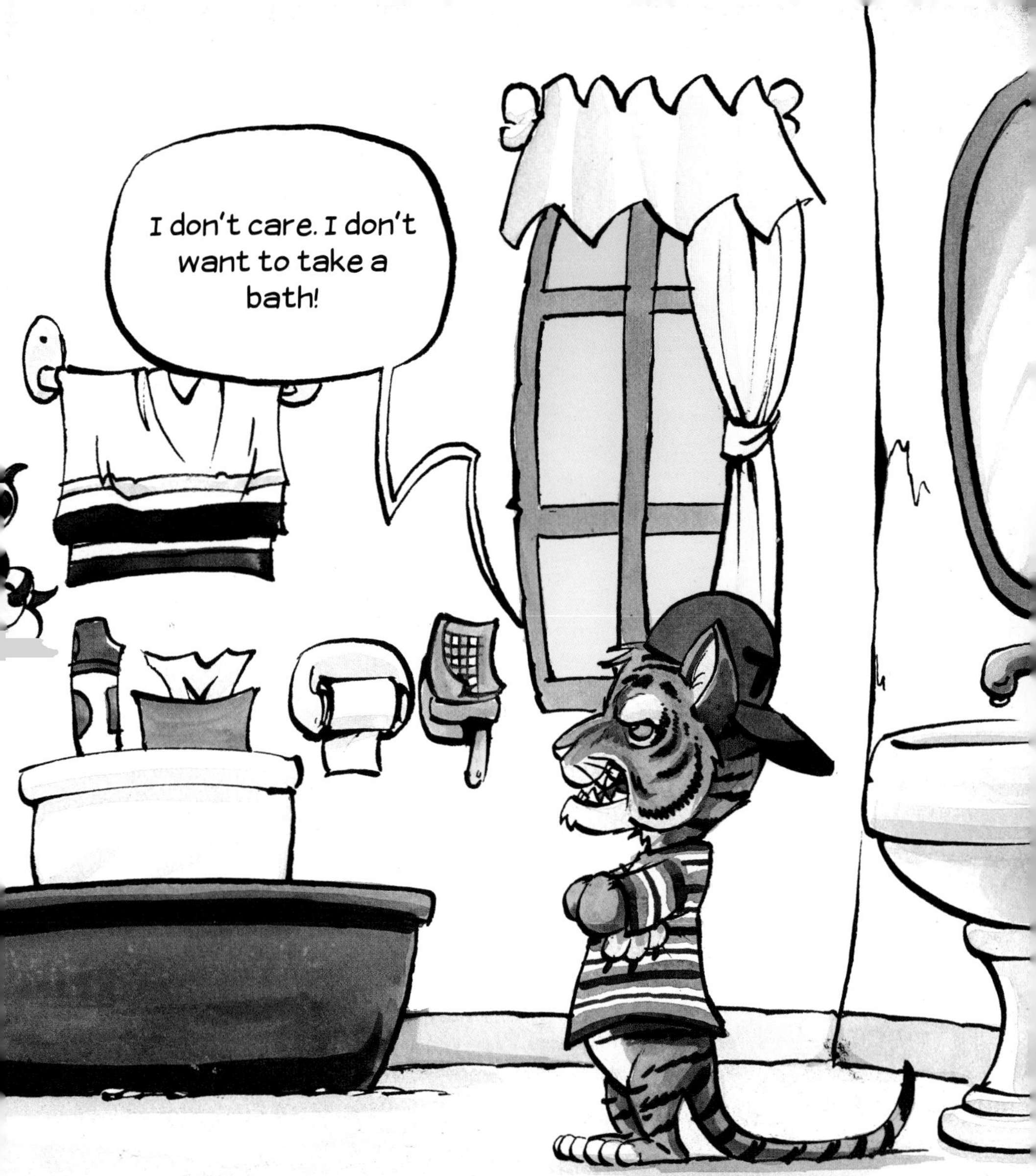
I don't care. I don't want to take a bath!

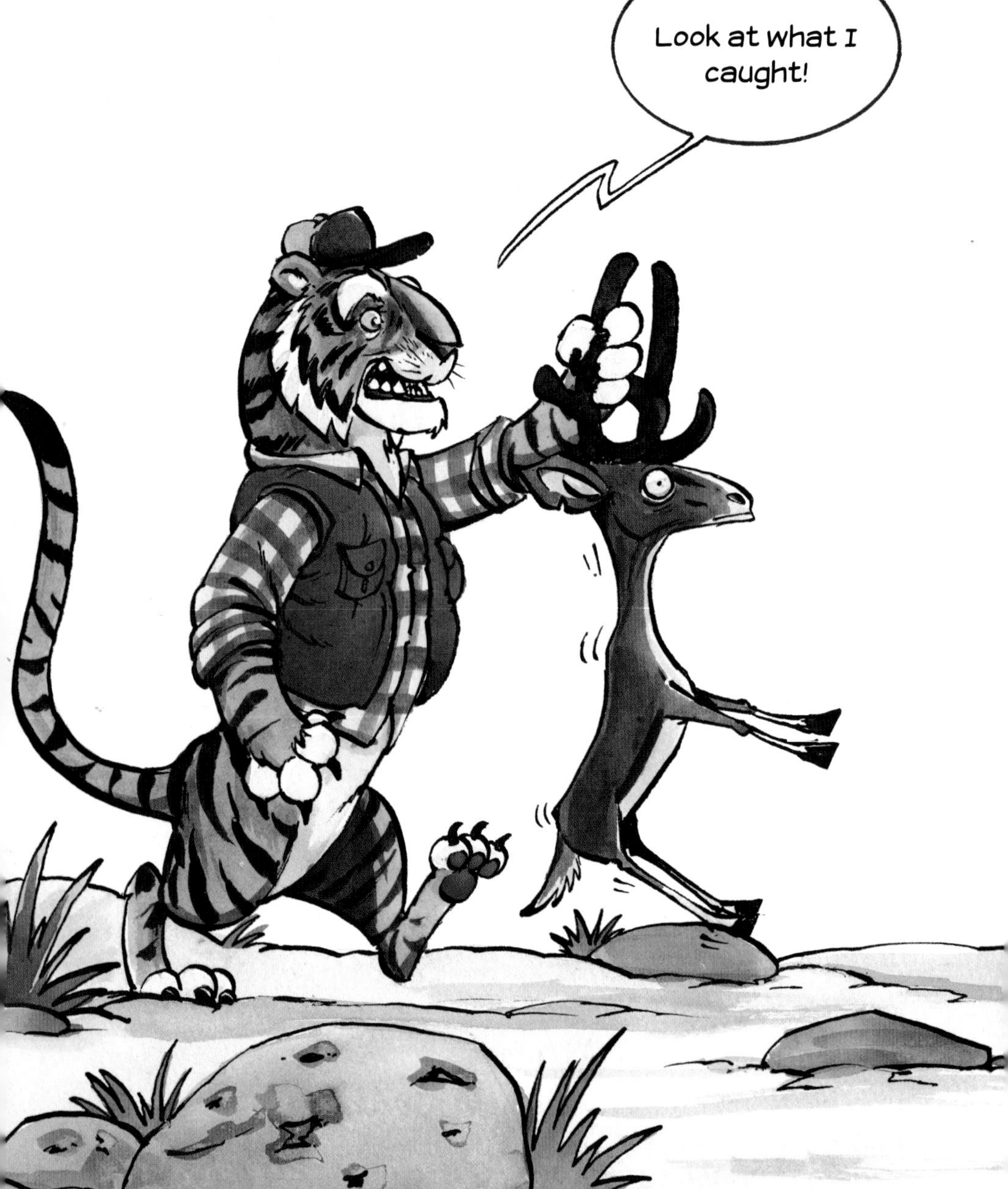
Look at what I caught!

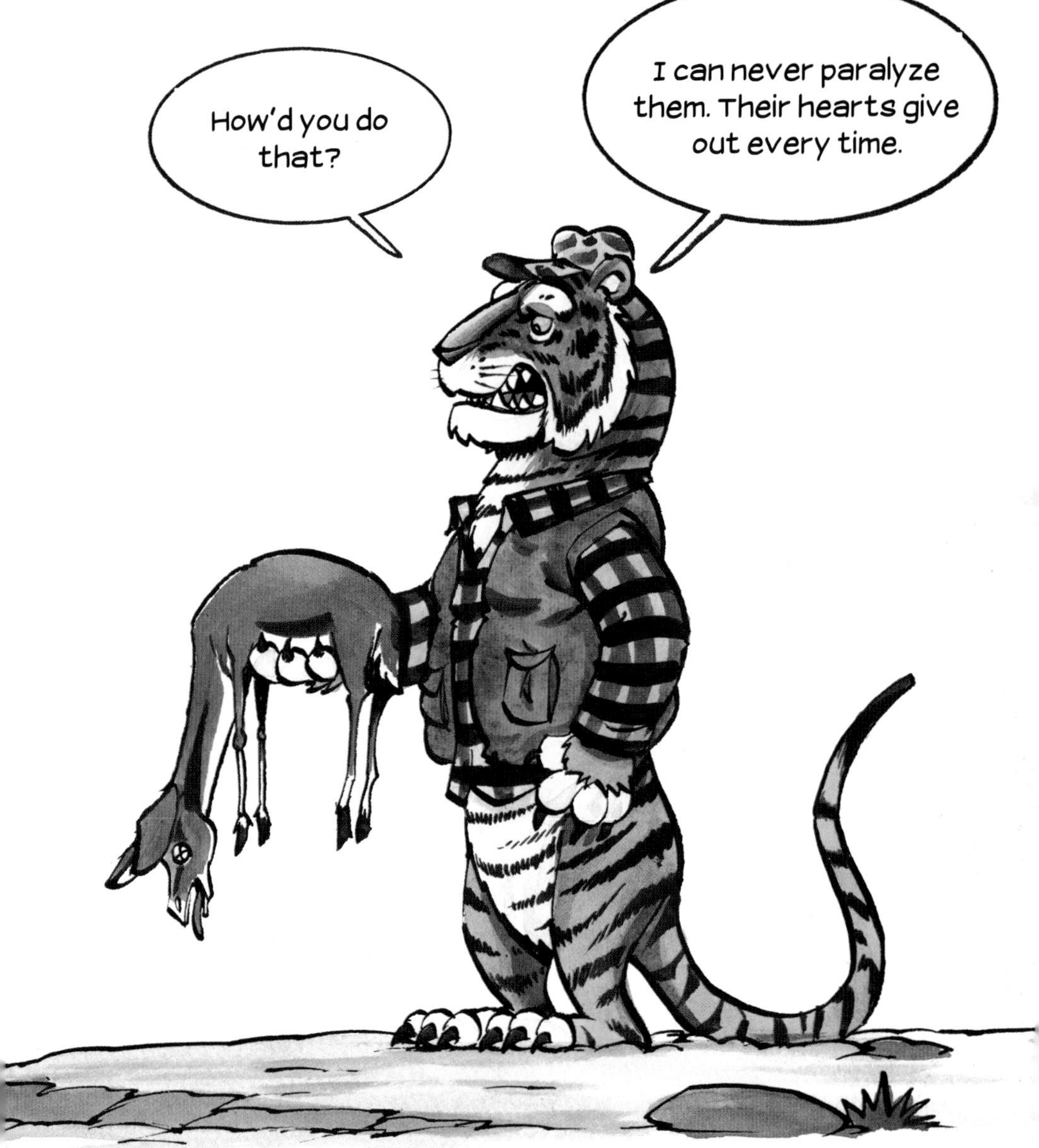
How'd you do that?
I can never paralyze them. Their hearts give out every time.

Tigers roar to keep other felines out of their territories and to scare and even paralyze their **prey**. You can hear a tiger roar from close to 3 kilometres (1.8 miles) away.

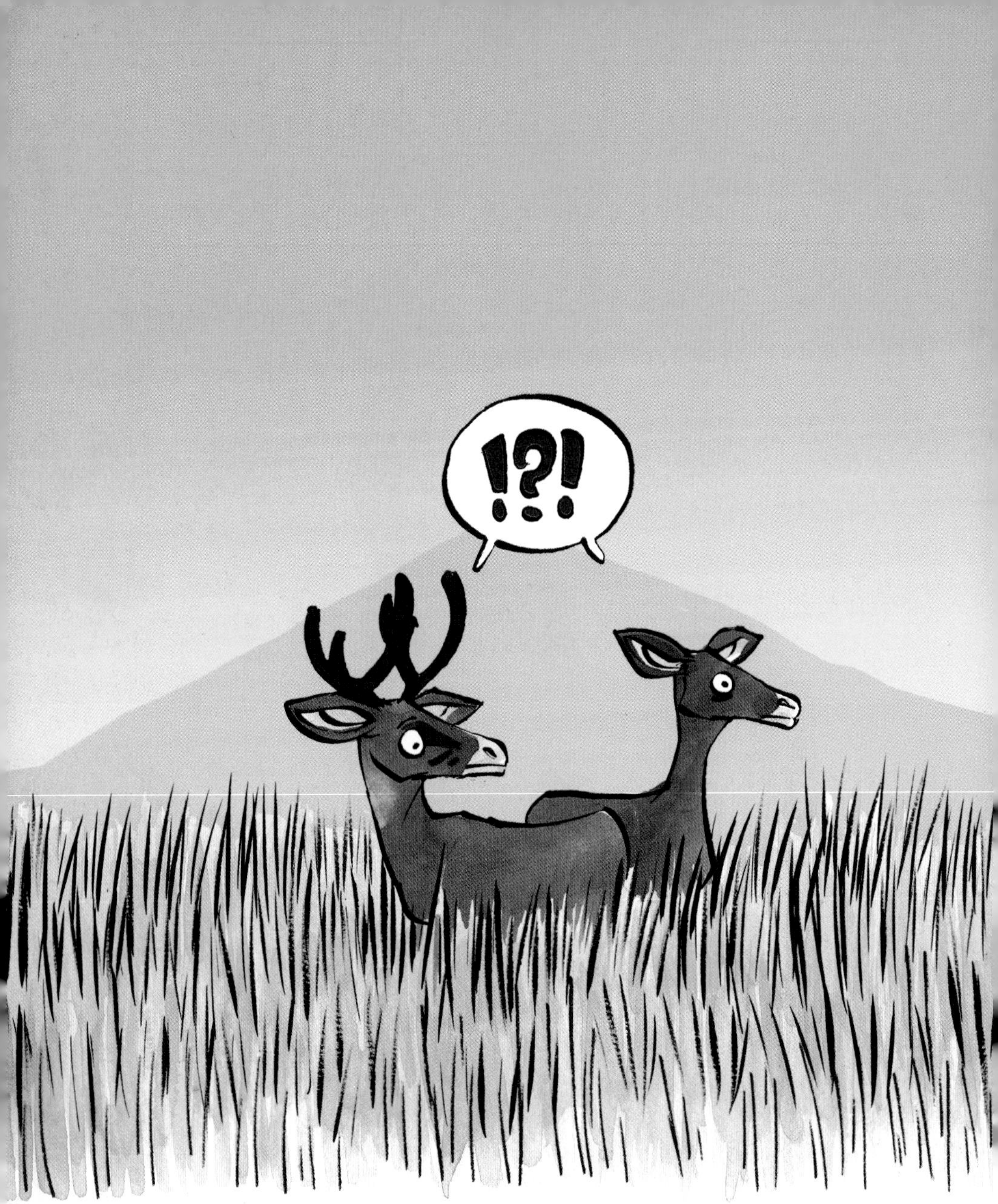
!?!

The tiger is a **solitary** hunter. Hiding within tall grasses, the tiger approaches its prey, belly to the ground. In just a few seconds, it attacks.

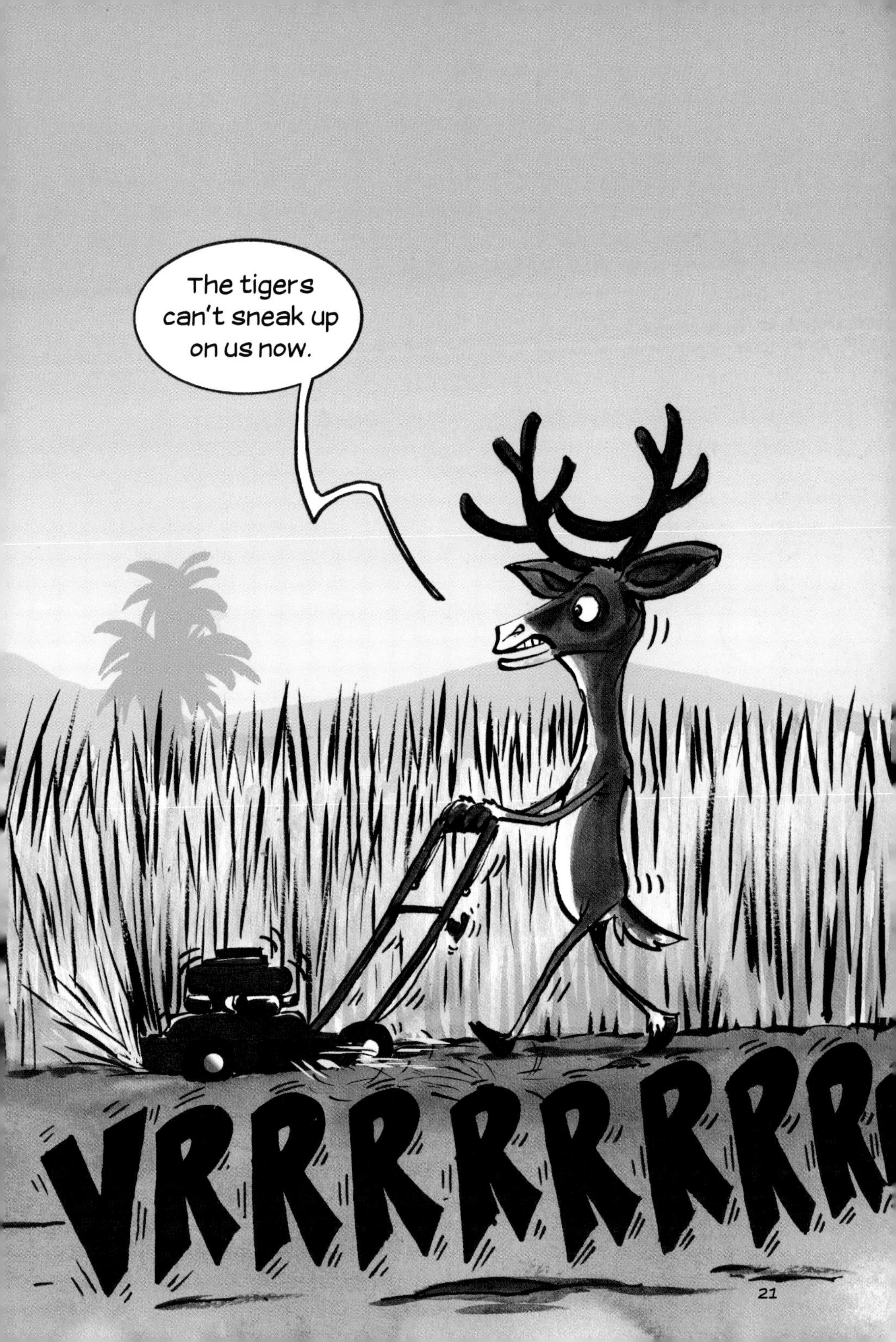
The tigers can't sneak up on us now.
VRRRRRRRRRR

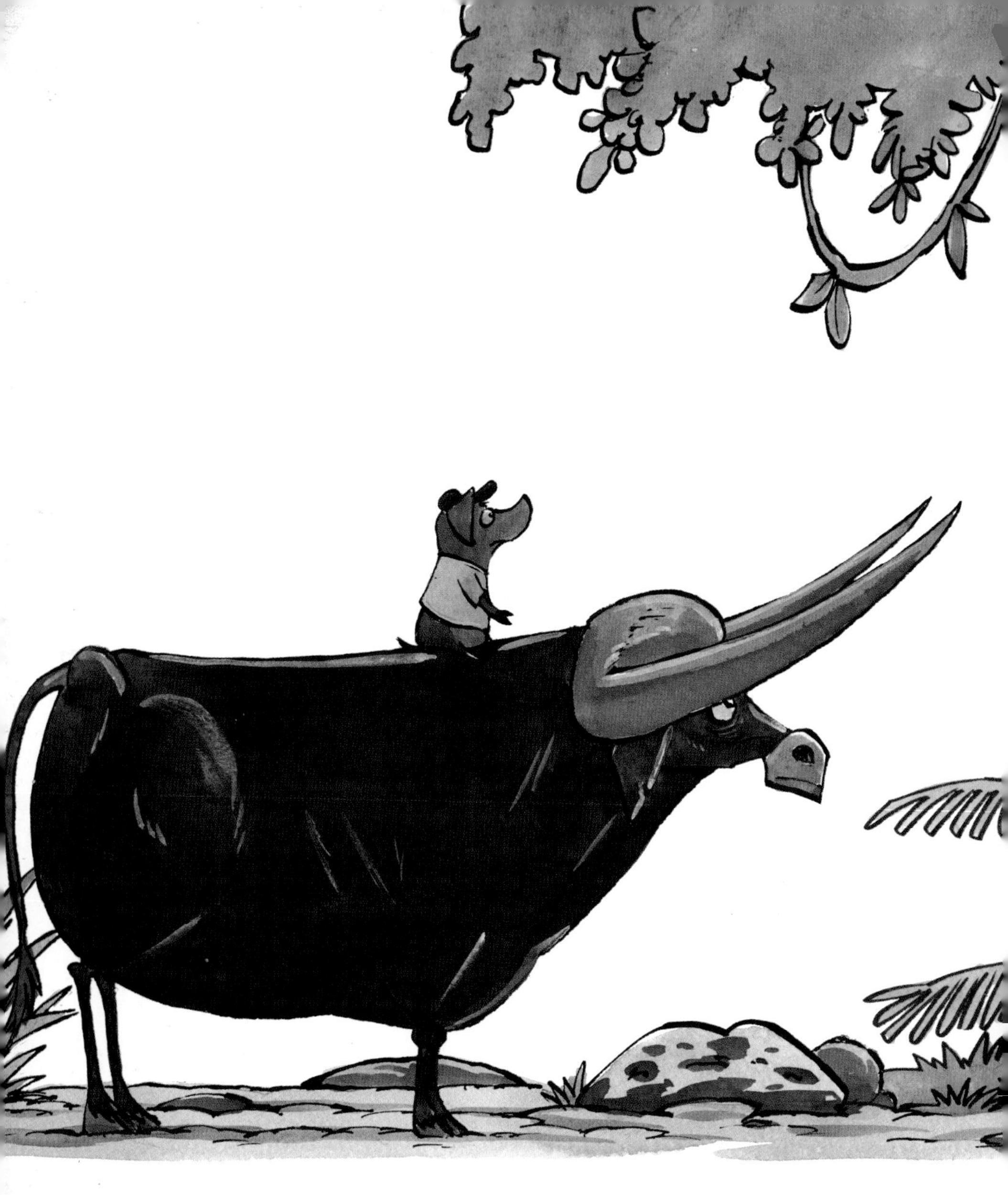

The tiger never attacks from up high, nor does it attack from far away.

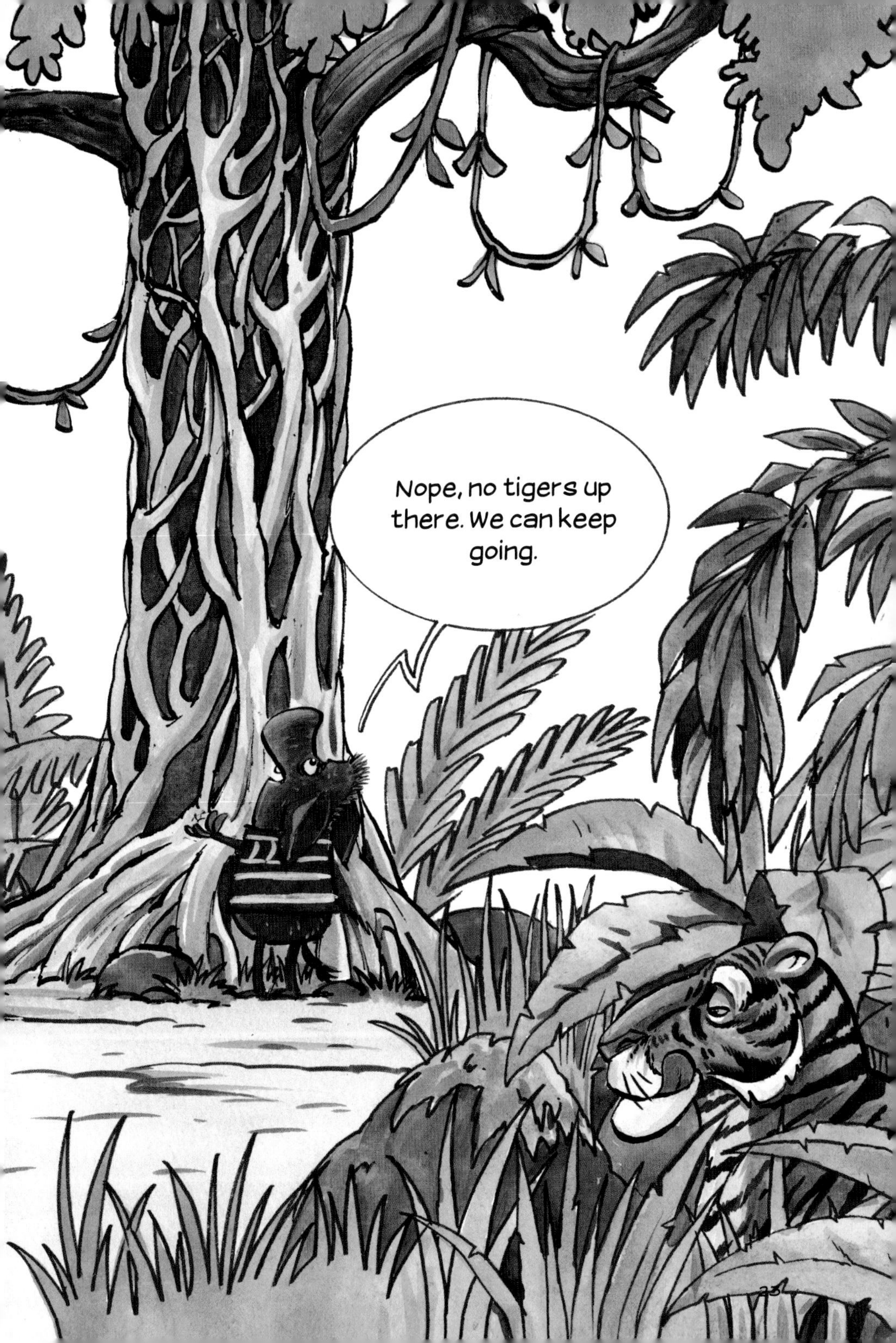
Nope, no tigers up there. We can keep going.

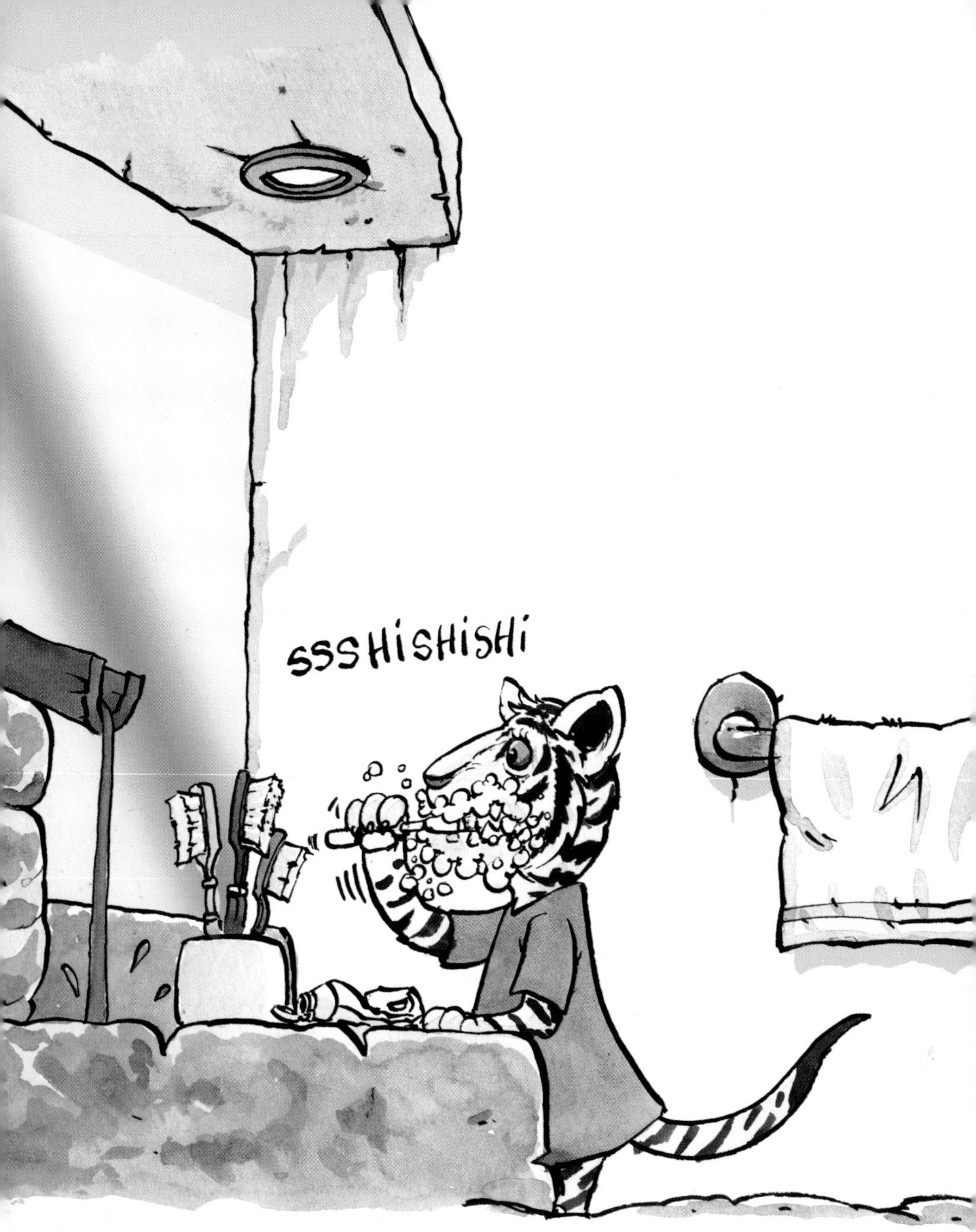
SSSHISHISHI

A tiger's fangs can reach 8 centimetres (3 inches) in length, which makes it one of the **terrestrial carnivores** with the longest teeth.

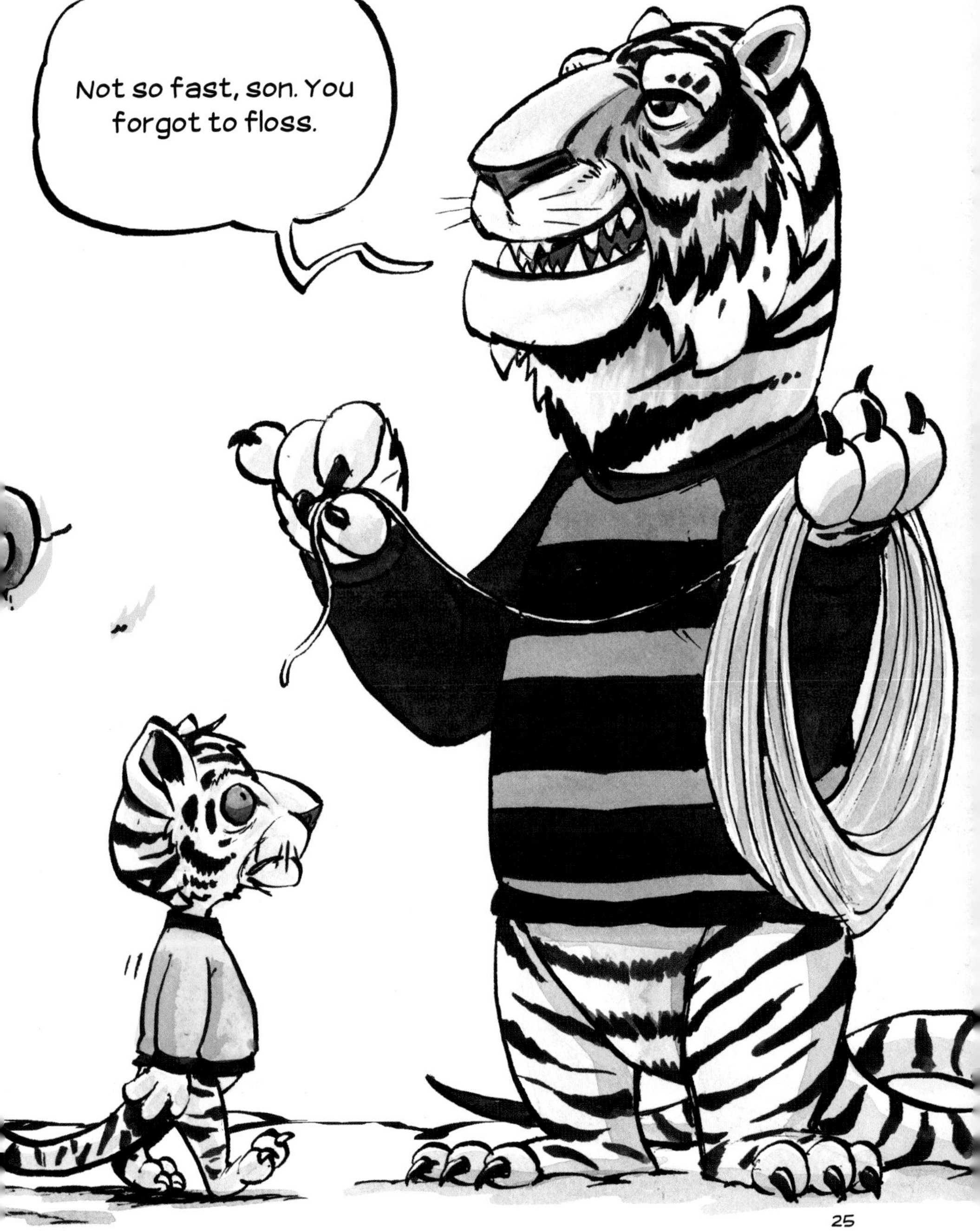
Not so fast, son. You forgot to floss.

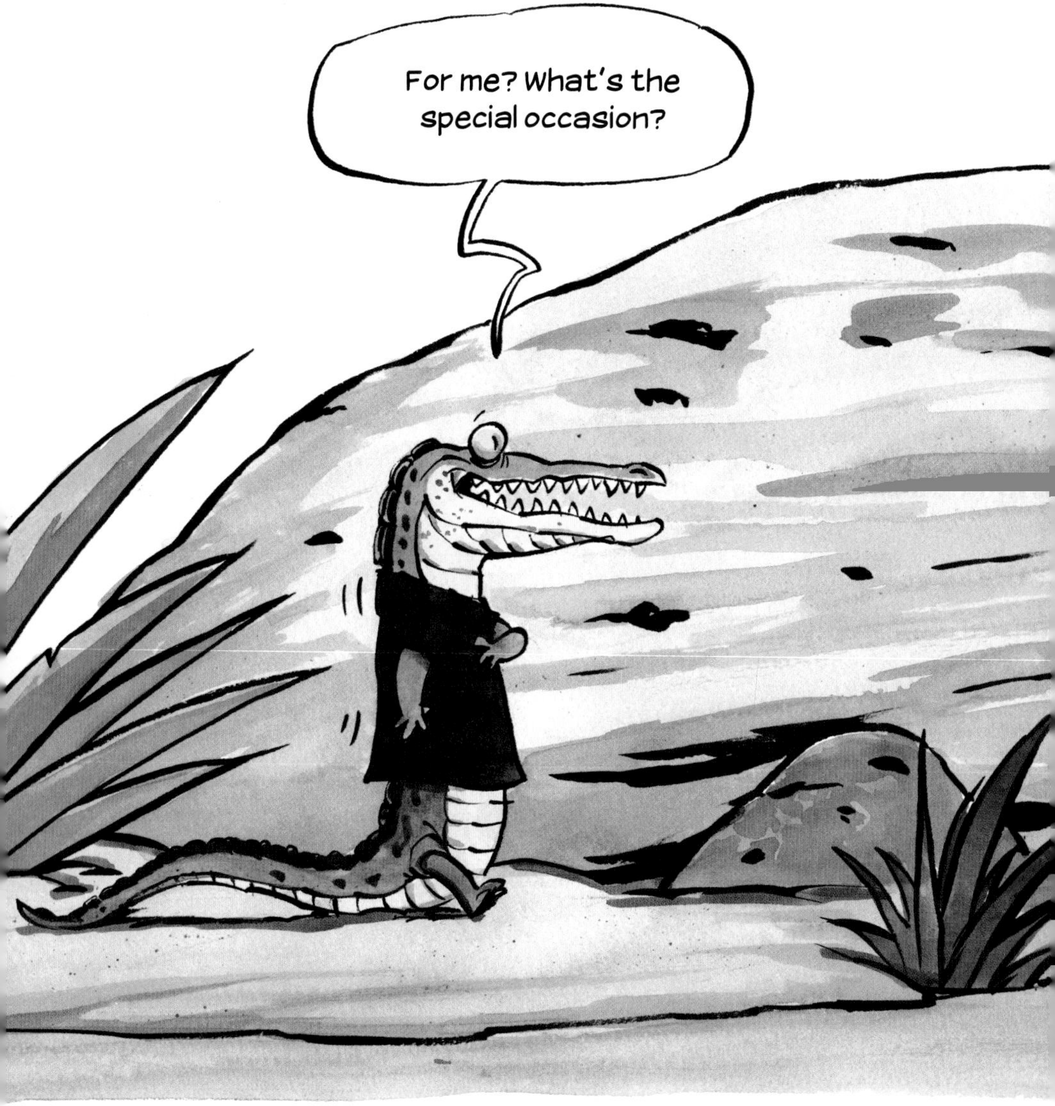
For me? What's the special occasion?

Tigers devour whatever they can catch. They mostly eat medium to large prey, such as elk, deer, buffalo, crocodiles, and wild boars.

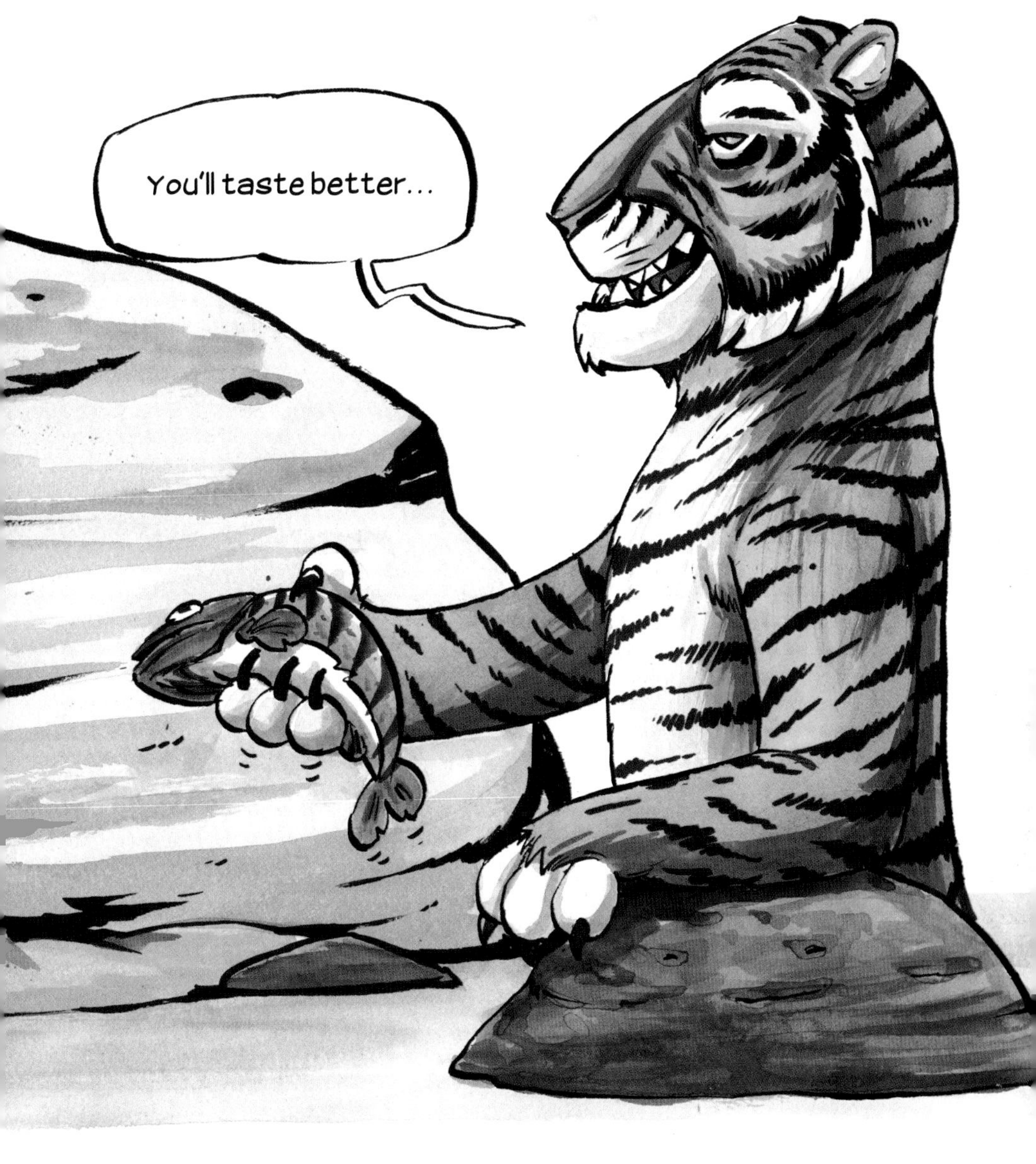
You'll taste better...

They sometimes catch young rhinoceros, baby elephants, and cattle, too.

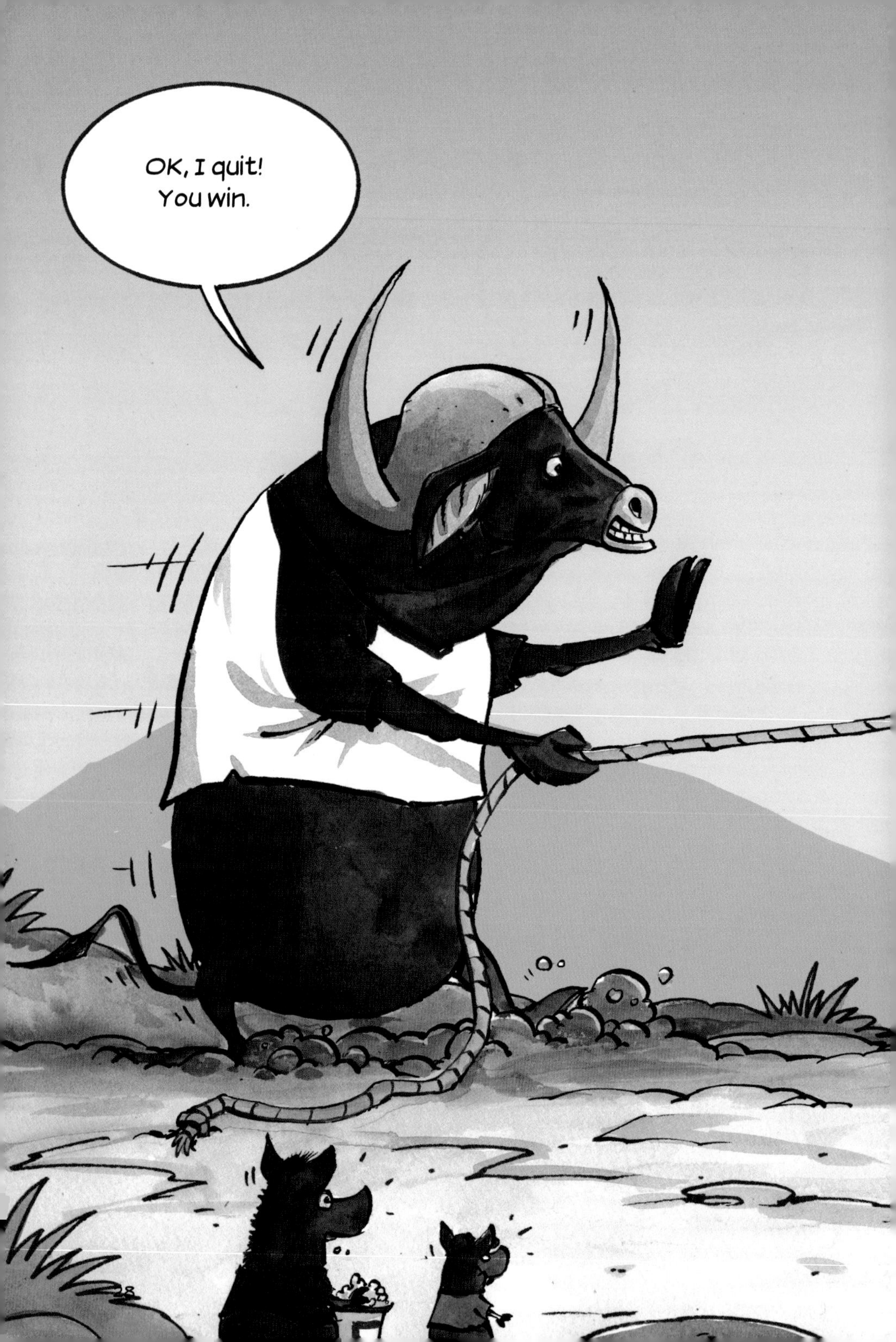
OK, I quit! You win.

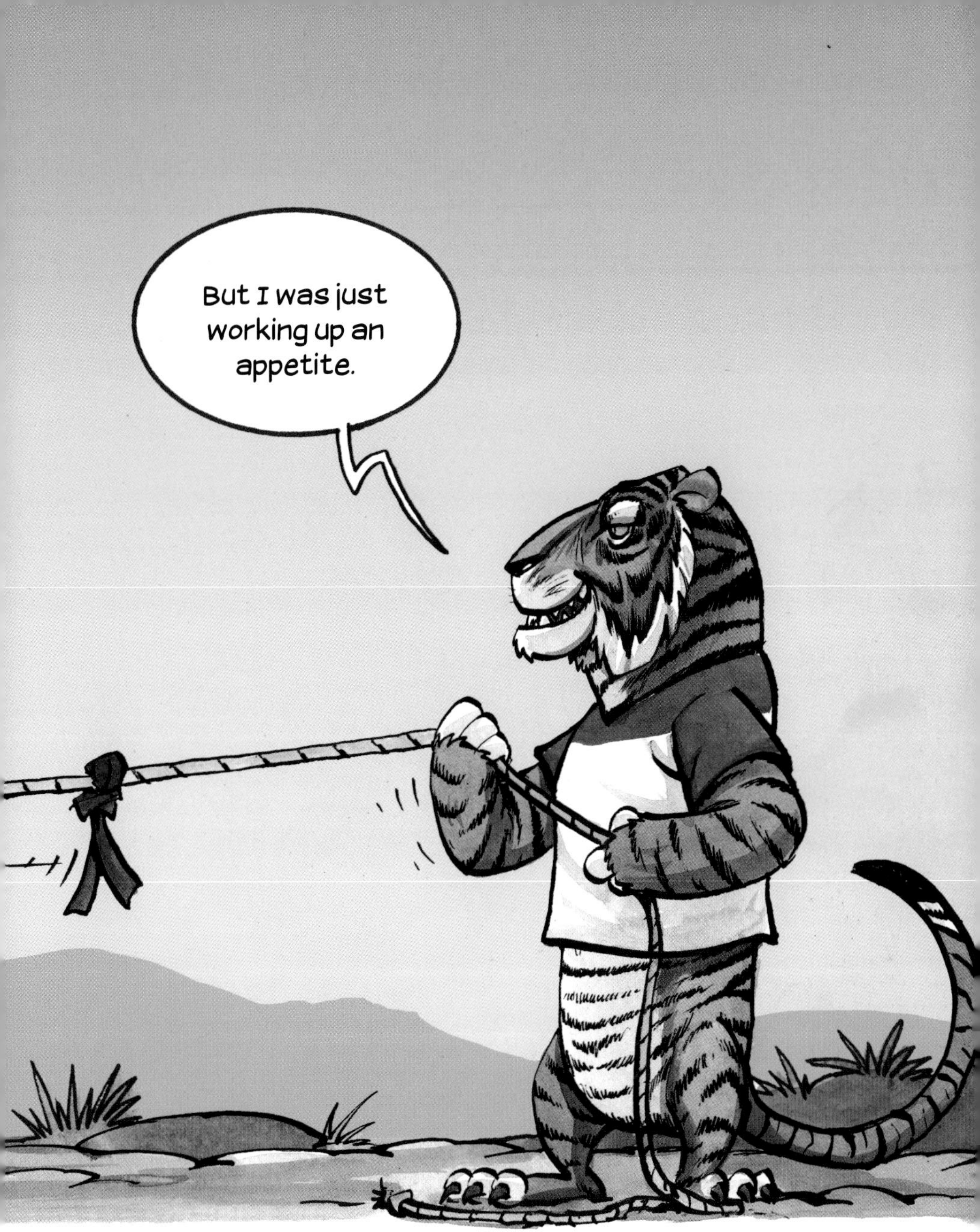
But I was just working up an appetite.

Endowed with Herculean strength, this powerful carnivore can drag a 900-kilogram (1,984-pound) prey by itself. By comparison, you would need 13 men to drag that much weight.

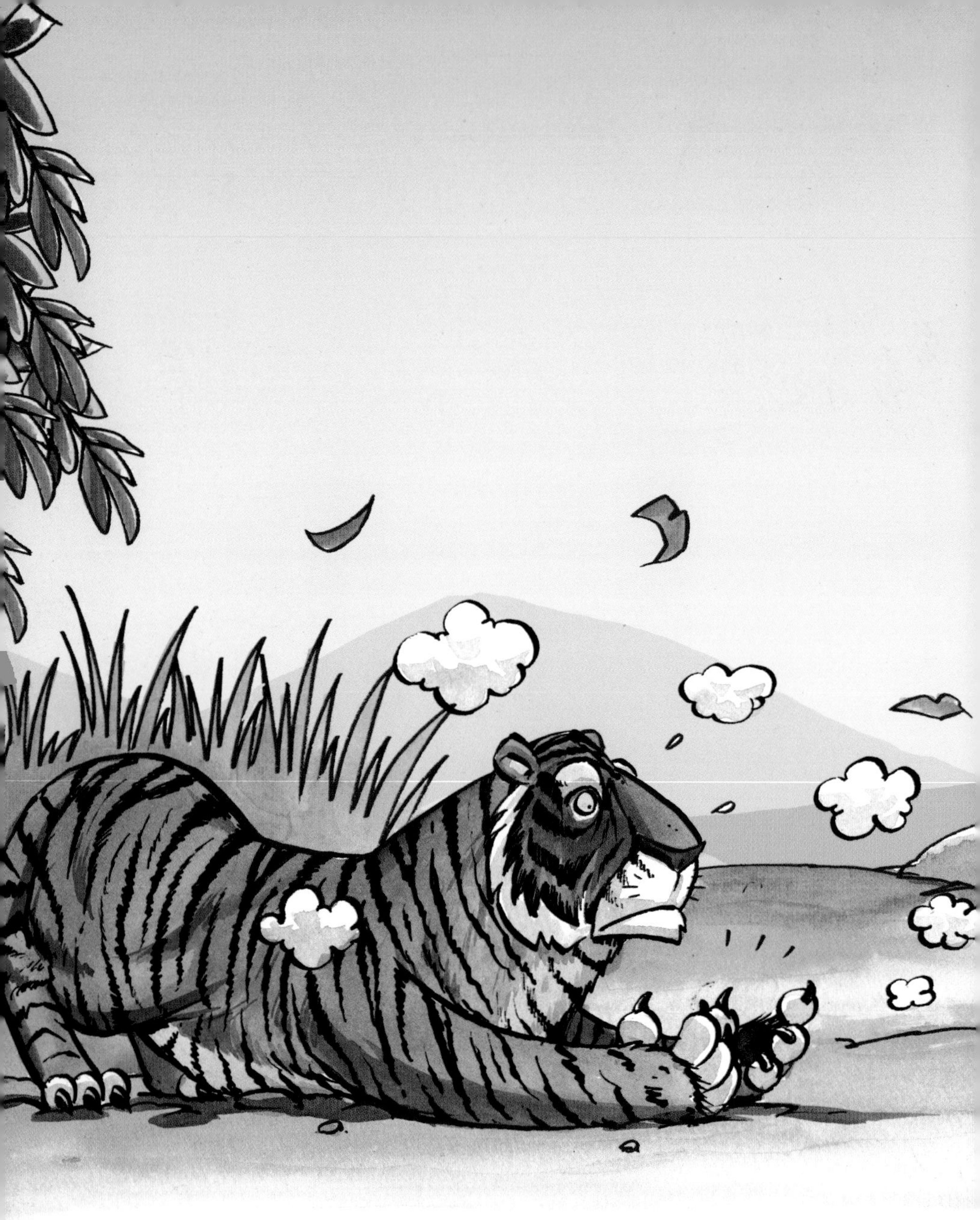

While hunting, tigers only successfully catch their prey 1 in 20 times.

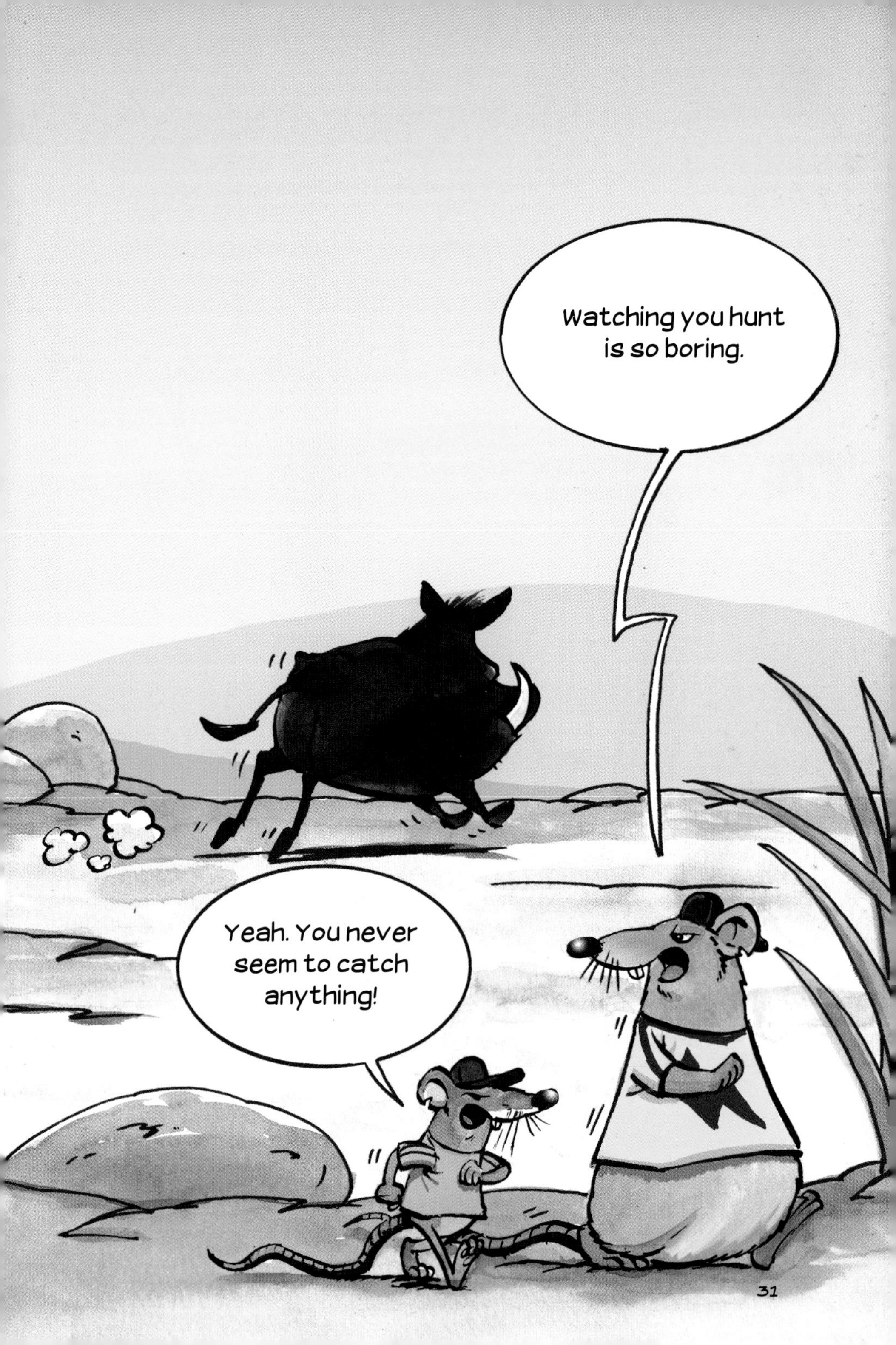
Watching you hunt is so boring.
Yeah. You never seem to catch anything!

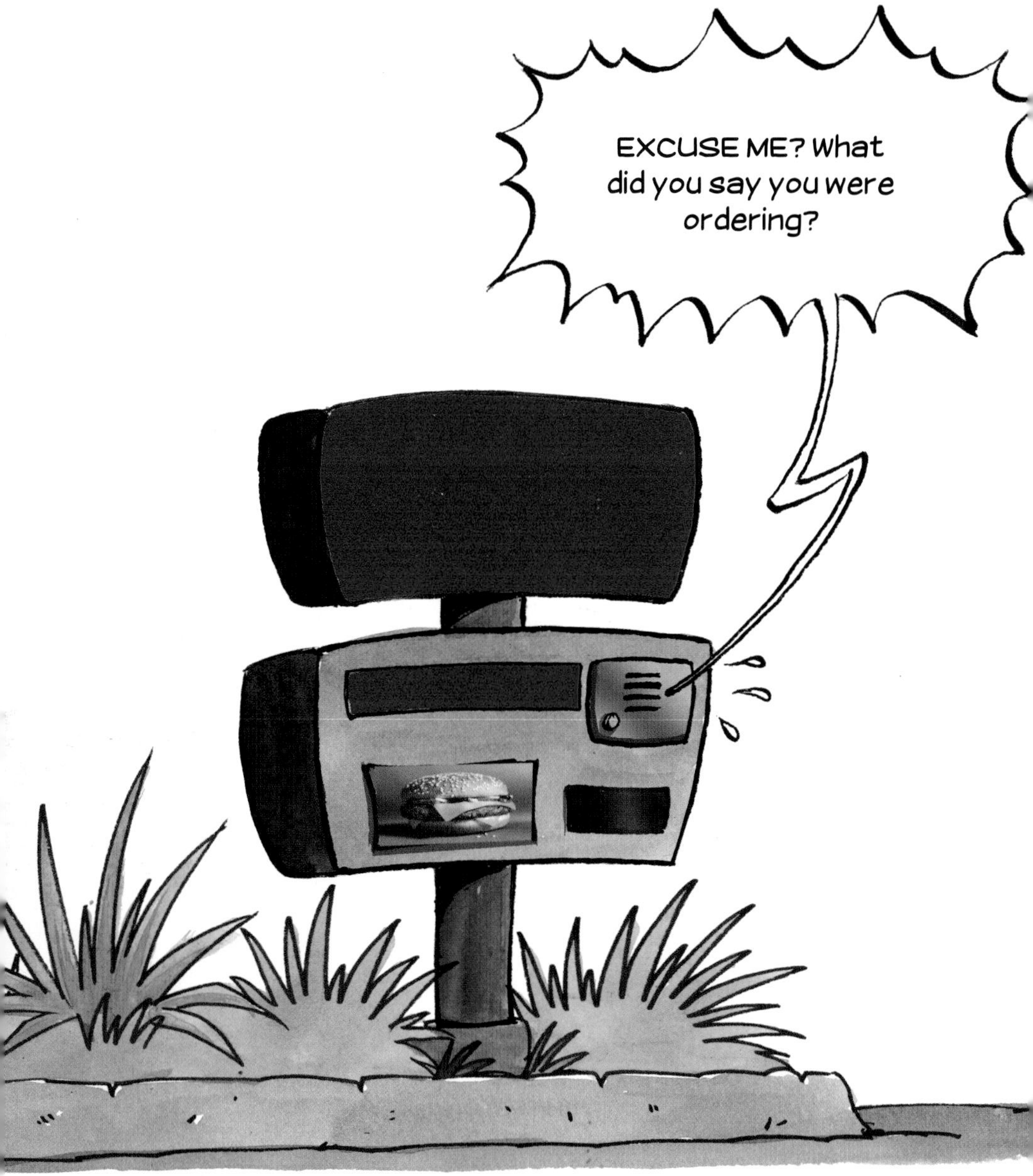
EXCUSE ME? What did you say you were ordering?

It is common for a tiger to eat 30 to 50 kilograms (65 to 110 pounds) of meat in a single meal.

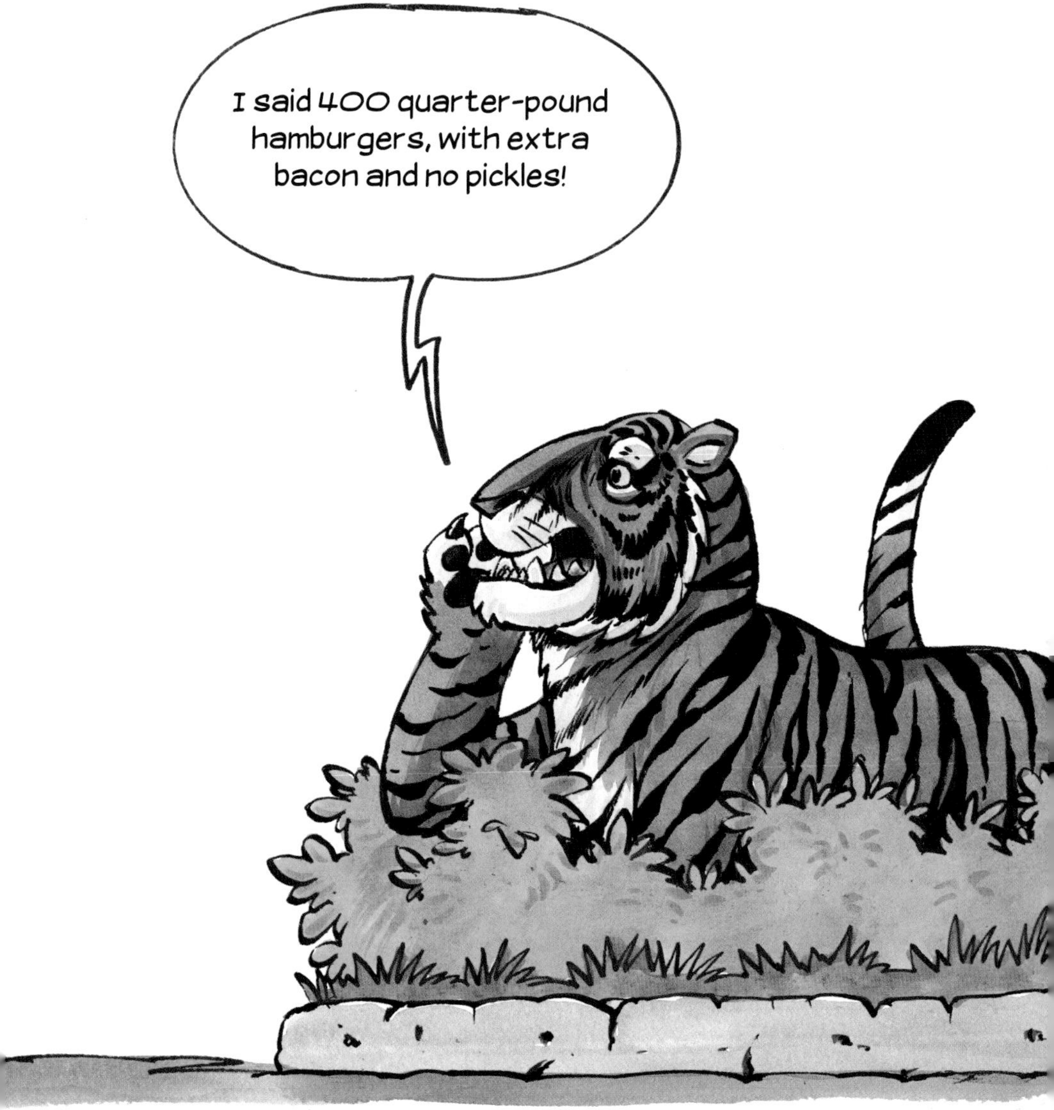
I said 400 quarter-pound hamburgers, with extra bacon and no pickles!

Since most tigers only catch one meal per week, they eat as much as they can while food is available.

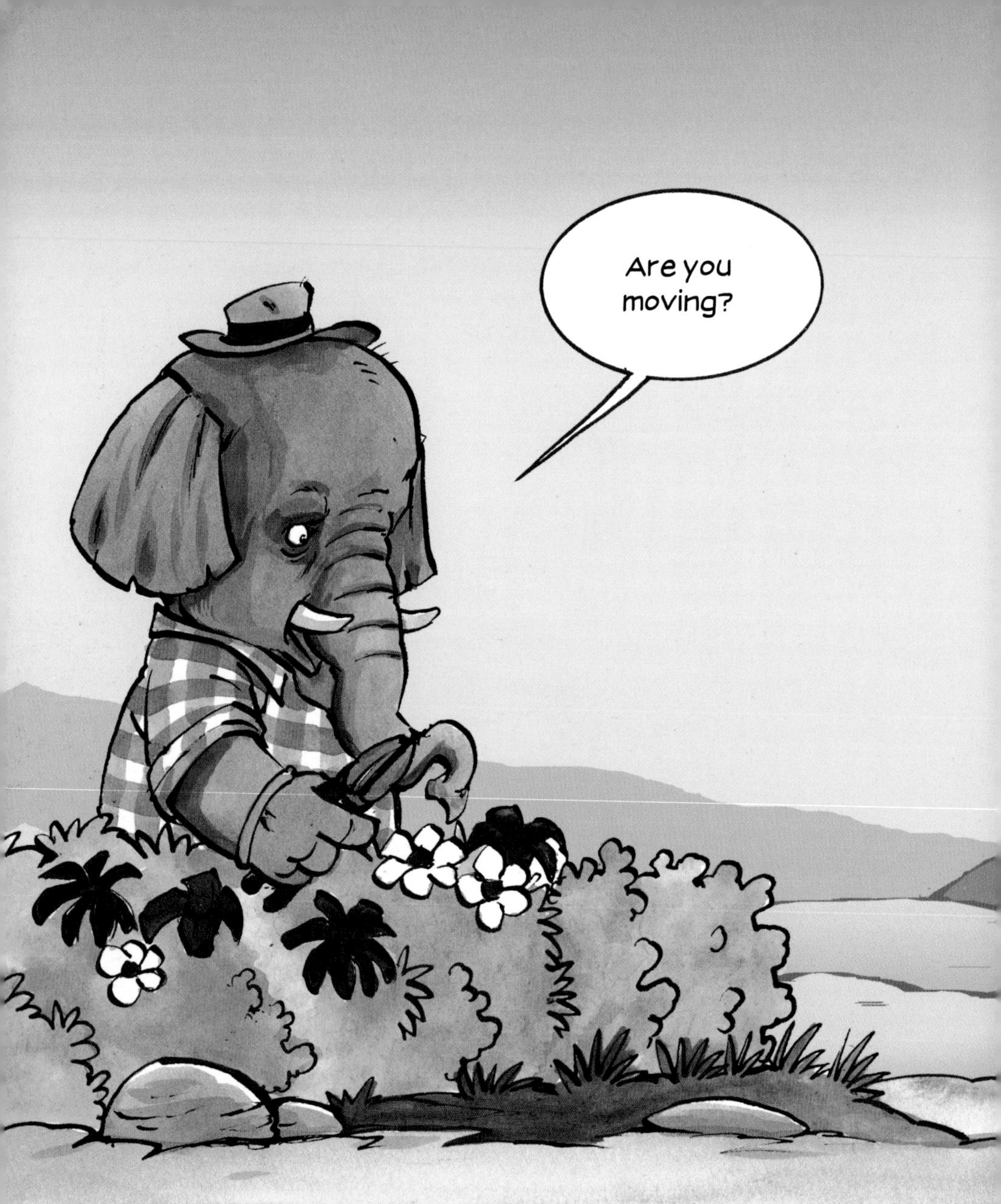
Are you
moving?

To survive, an adult tiger must ingest approximately 2,300 kilograms (5,070 pounds) of food every year. That figure represents about 45 kilograms (99 pounds) per week.

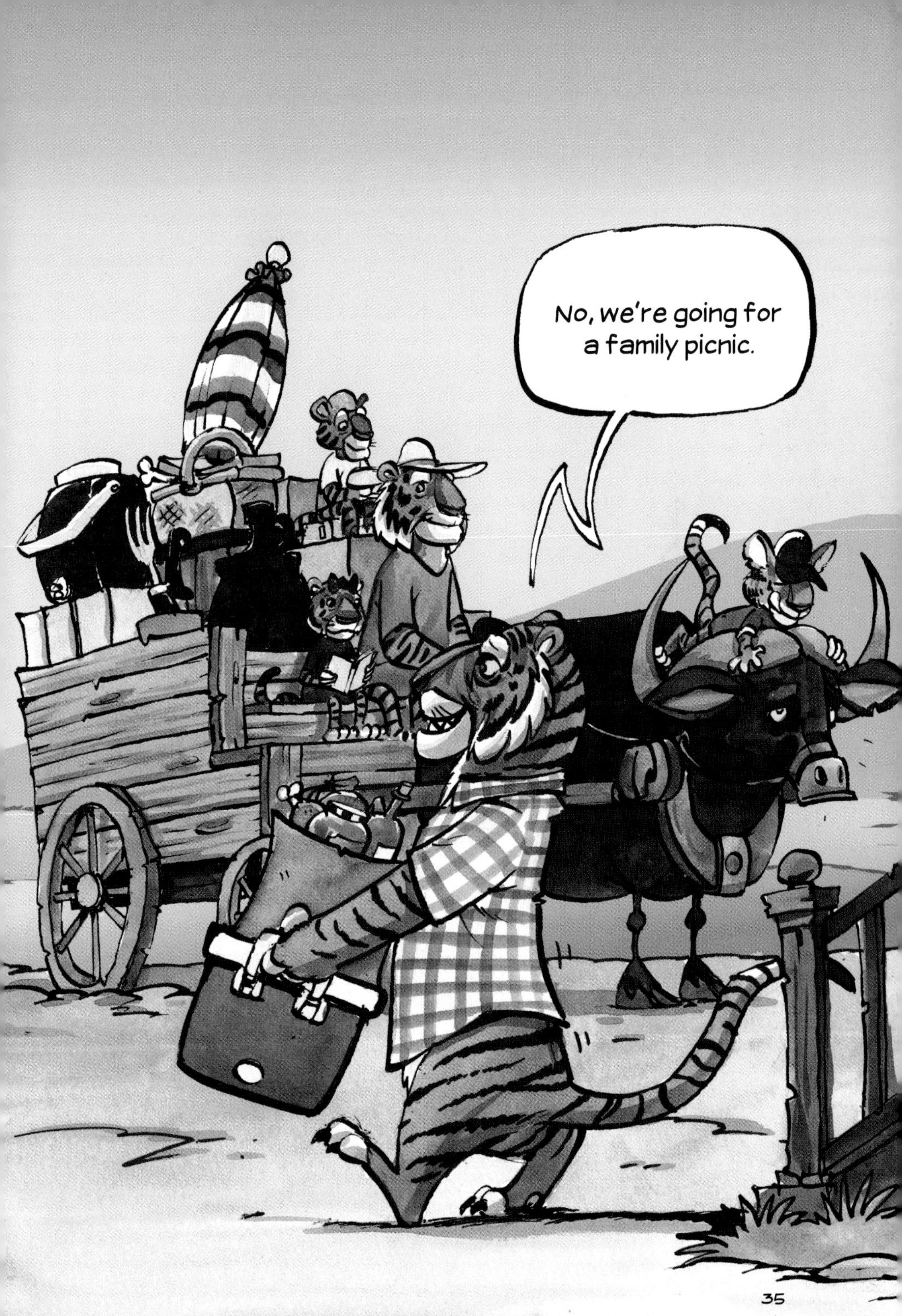
No, we're going for a family picnic.

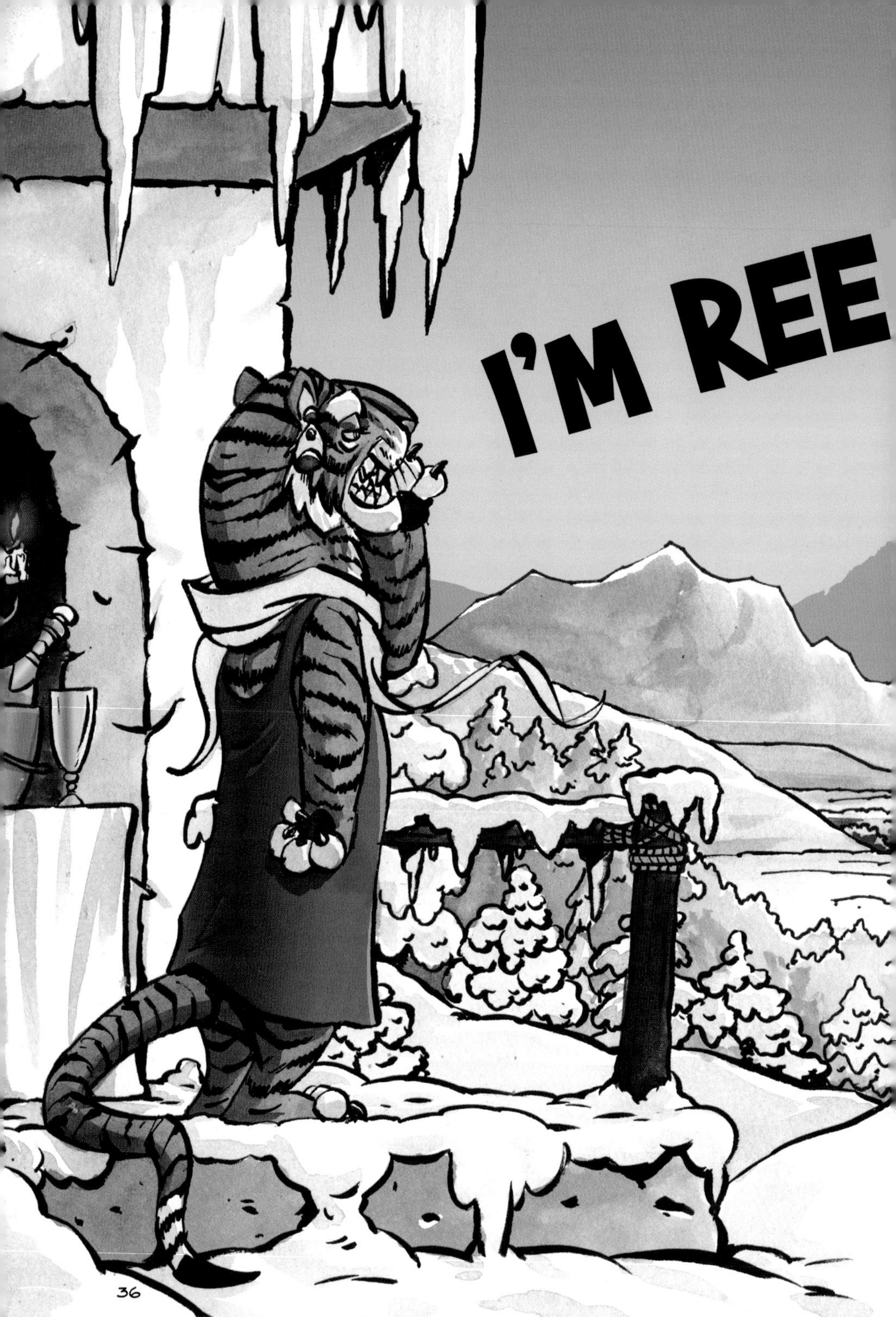
I'M REE

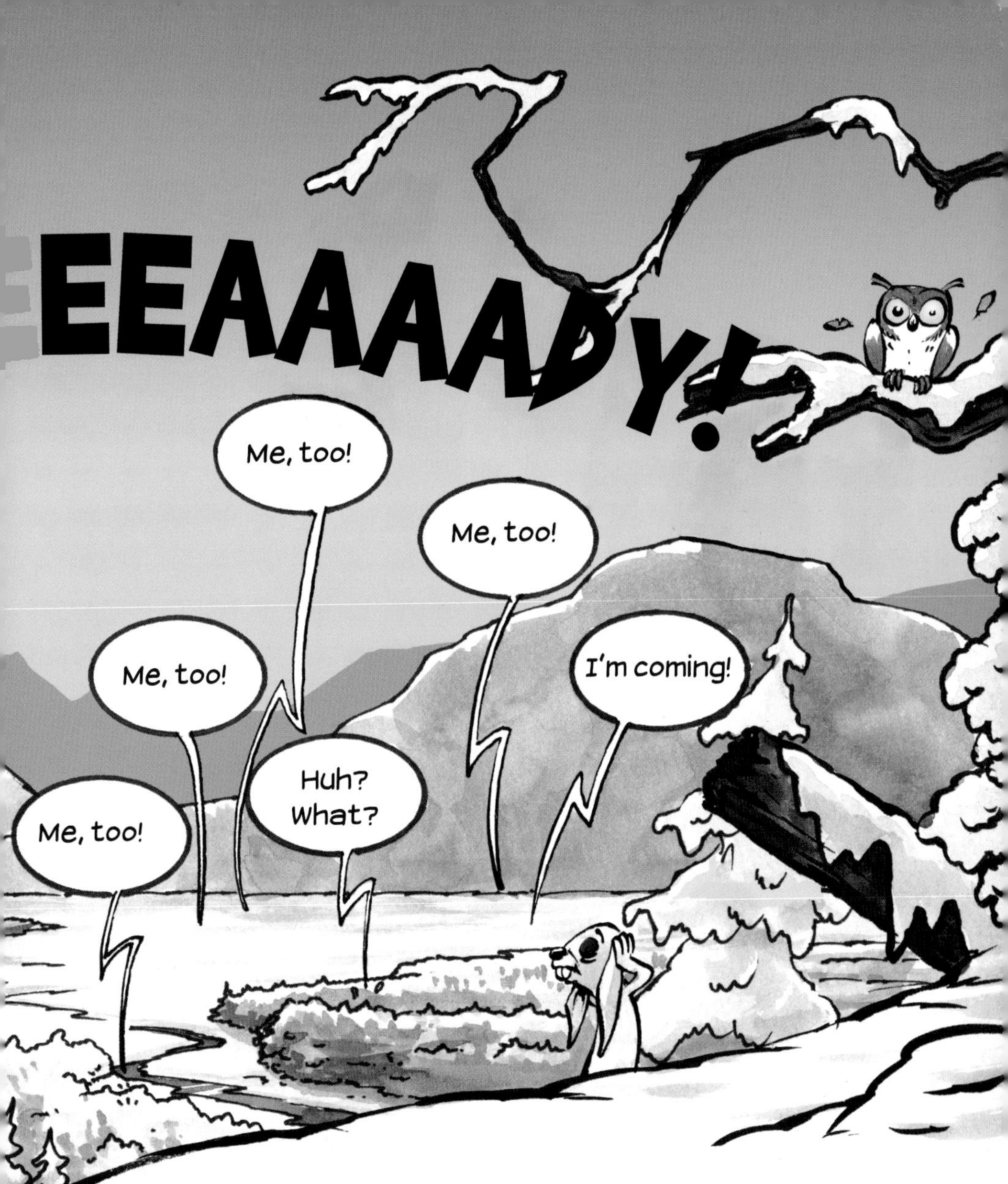
EEAAAADY!
Me, too!
Me, too!
Me, too!
I'm coming!
Huh?
What?
Me, too!

Tigers are generally solitary creatures. Males and females rarely meet up. During mating season, females emit a particular sound to attract the males. The sound can be heard from over 2 kilometres (1.2 miles) away.

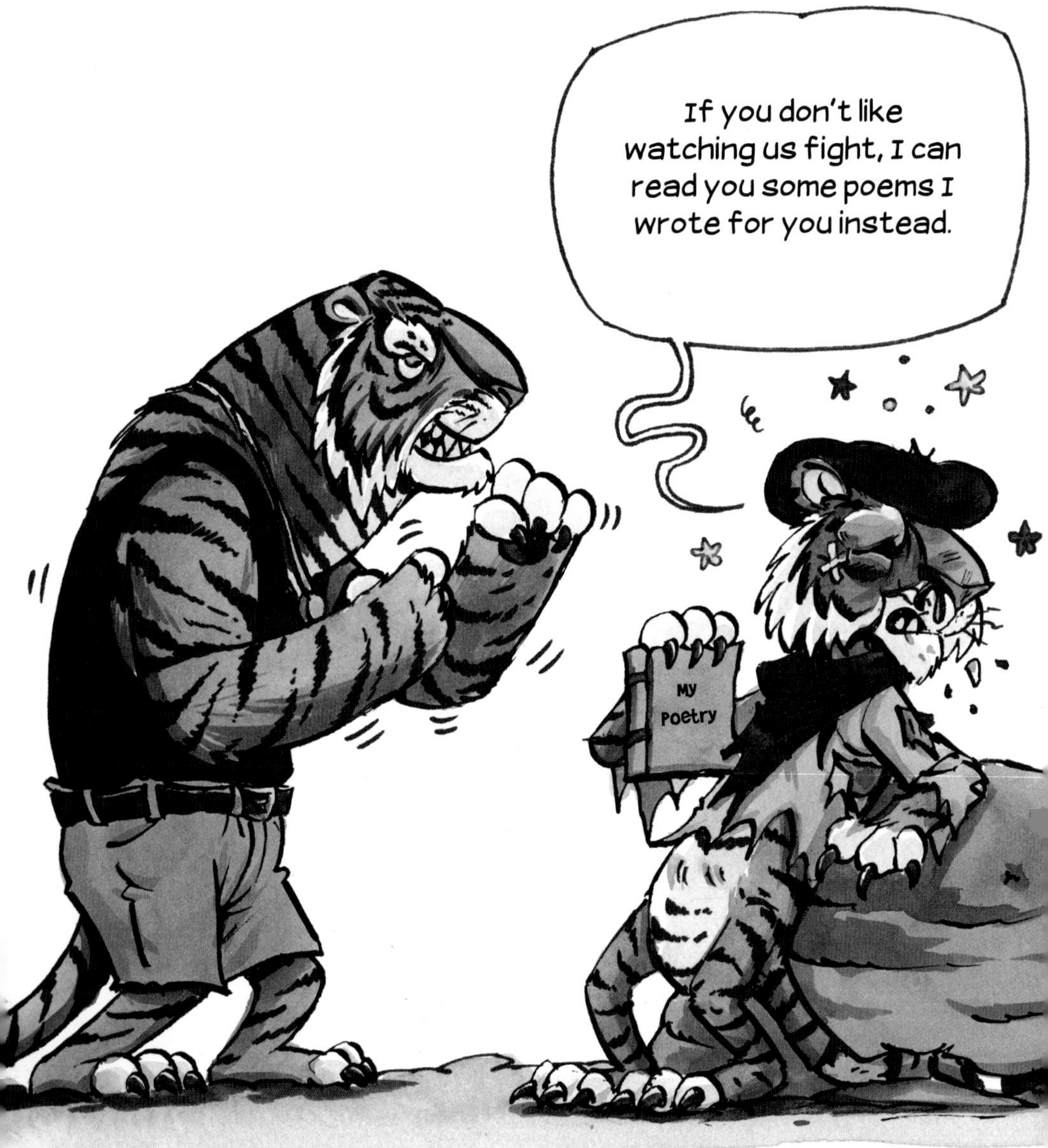
If you don't like watching us fight, I can read you some poems I wrote for you instead.
My Poetry

Tigers mate for approximately 5 days. Males will often fight each other for the chance to mate with a female.

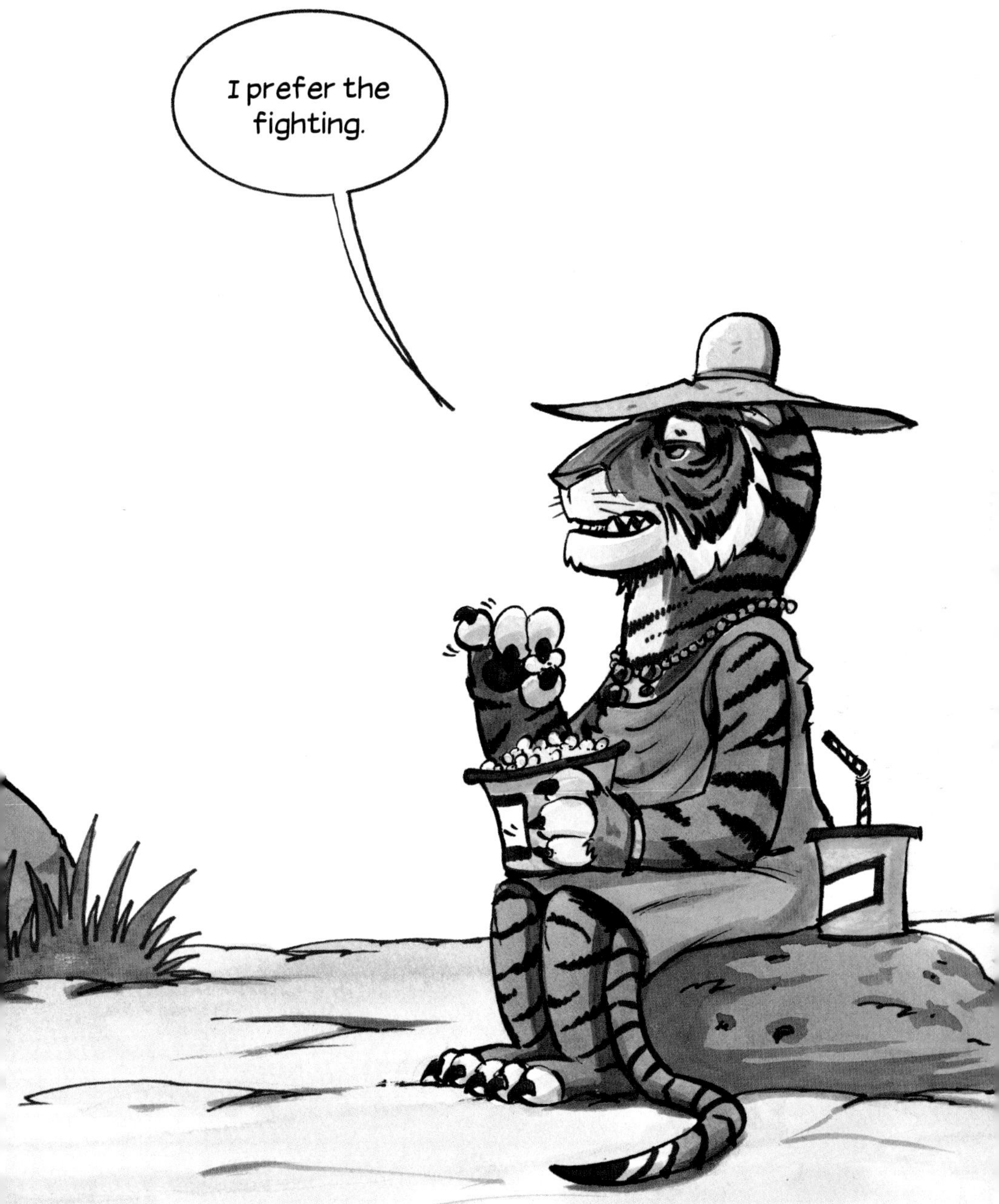
I prefer the fighting.

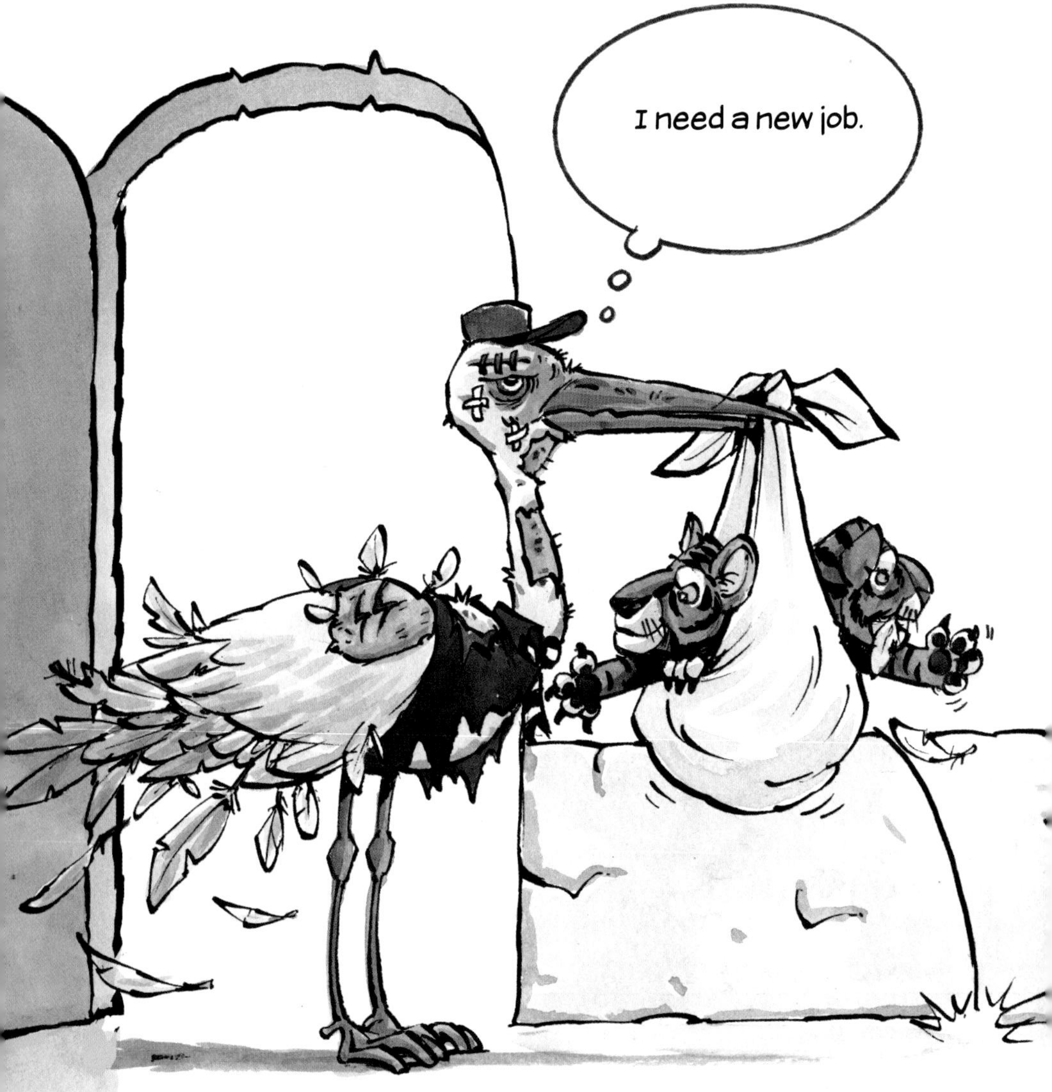
I need a new job.

After 15 to 16 weeks of pregnancy, the tigress will give birth to 2, 3, or 4 cubs.

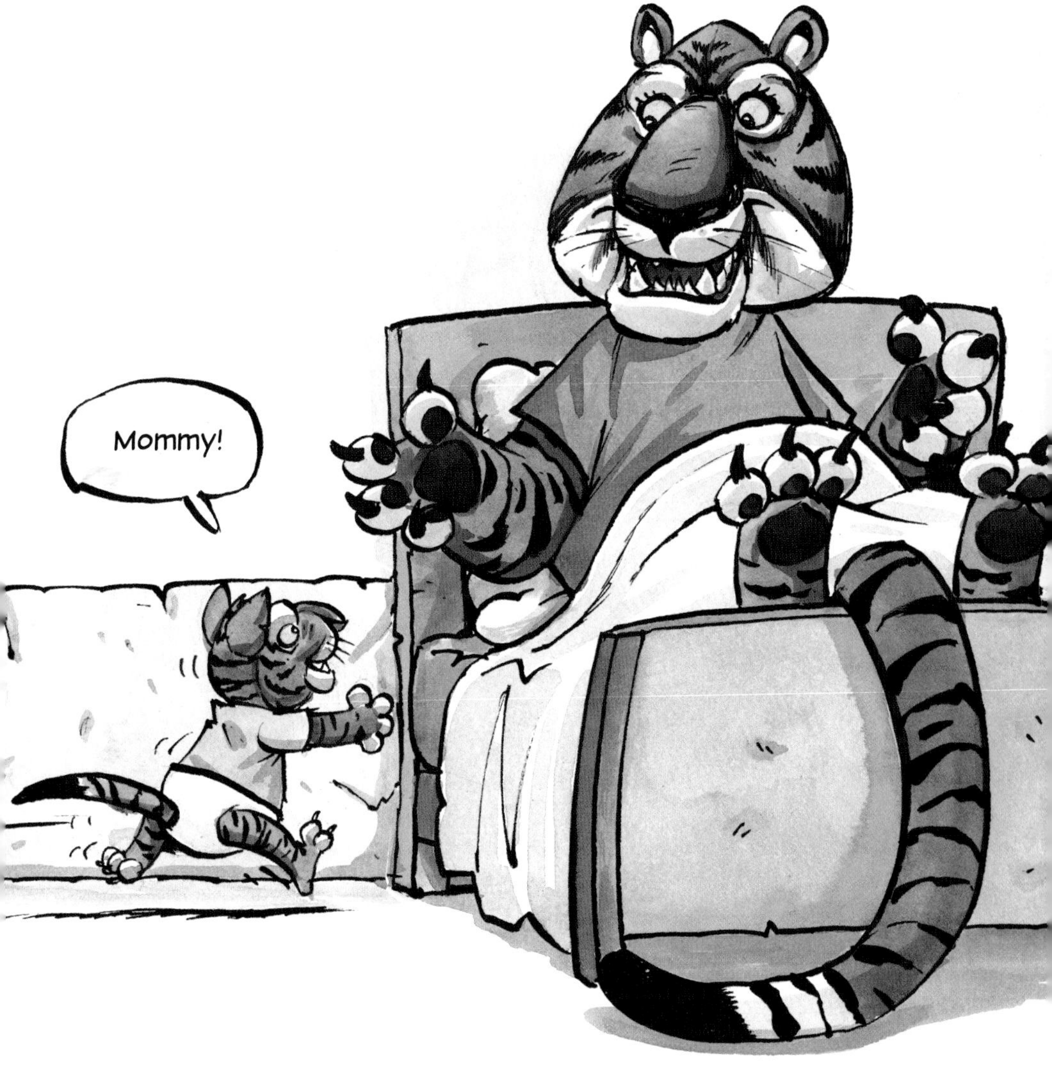
Mommy!

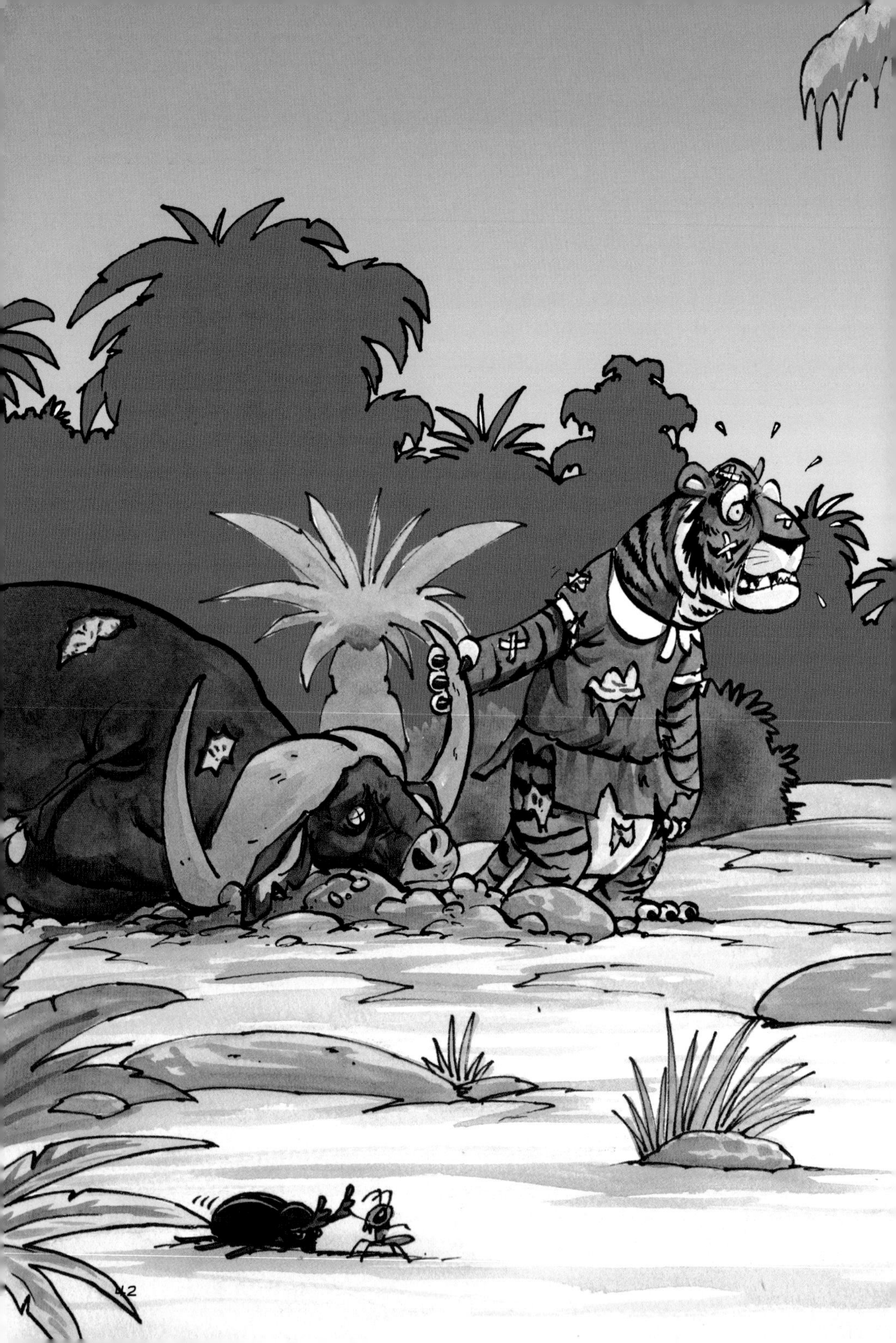

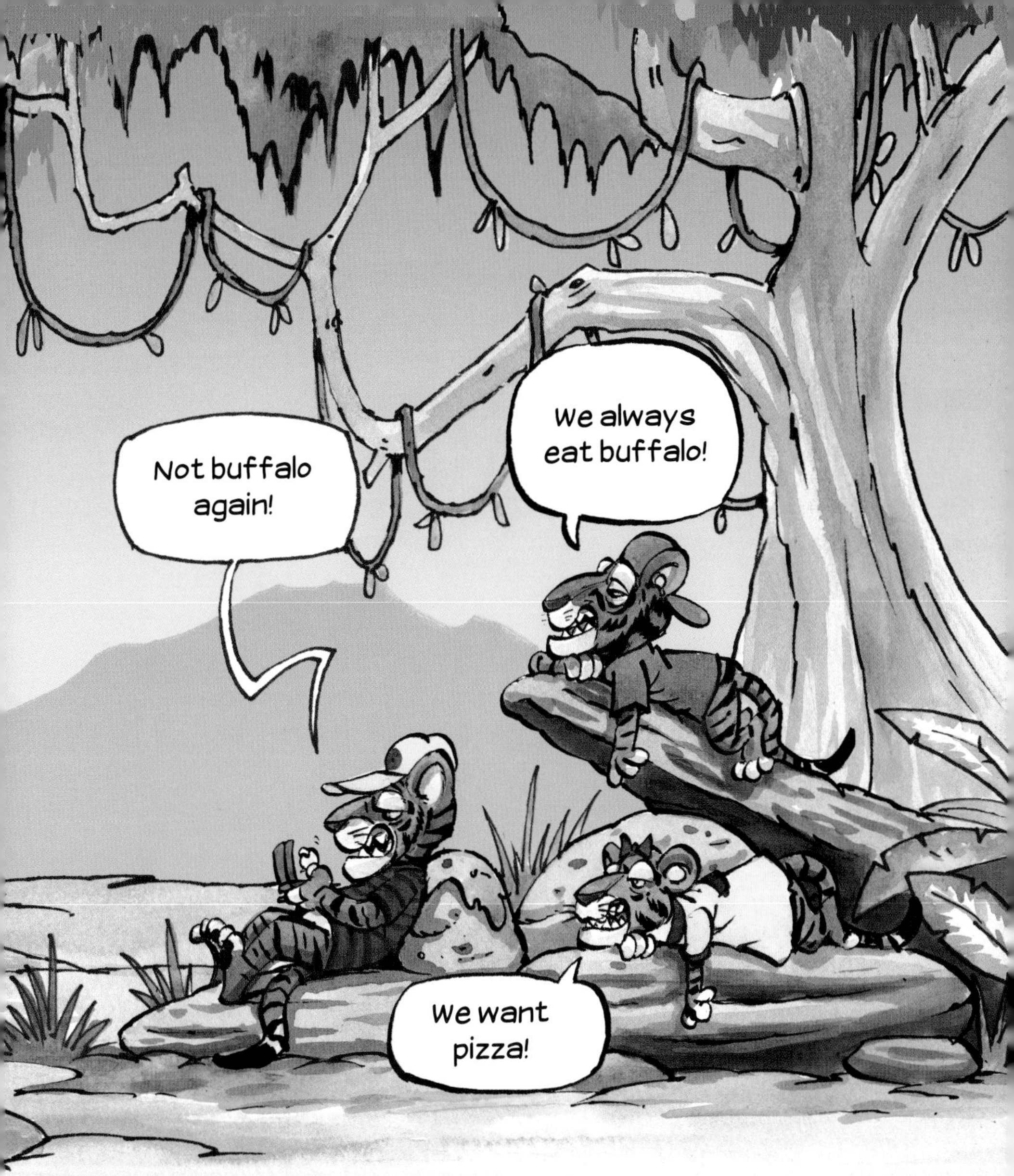
Not buffalo again!
We always eat buffalo!
We want pizza!

Tiger cubs begin to follow their mother after 8 weeks. They will be dependent on her until approximately 2 years of age.

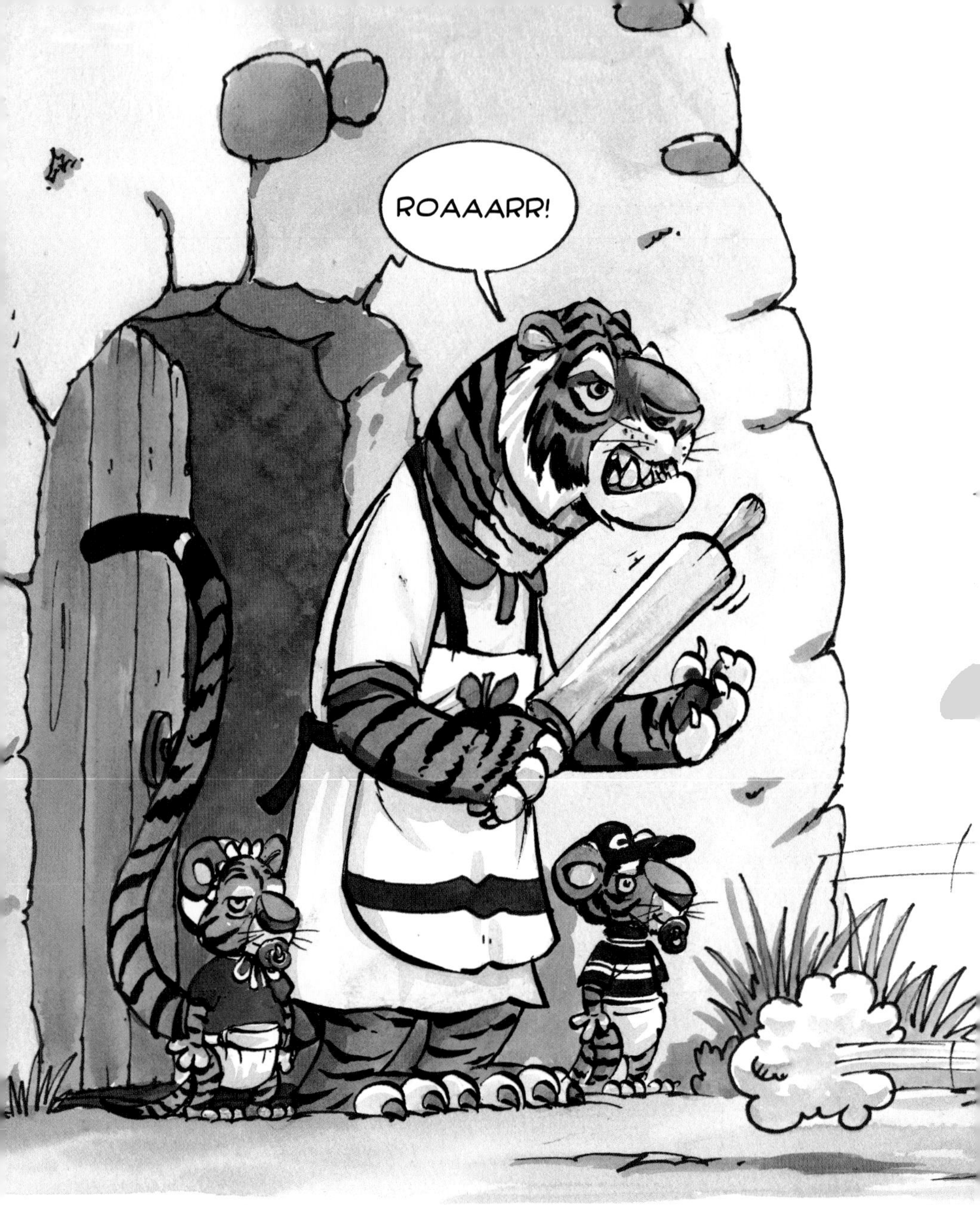
ROAAARR!

Female tigers raise their cubs alone. They are particularly wary of males, since they have a tendency to attack cubs, especially those that are under 6 months of age.

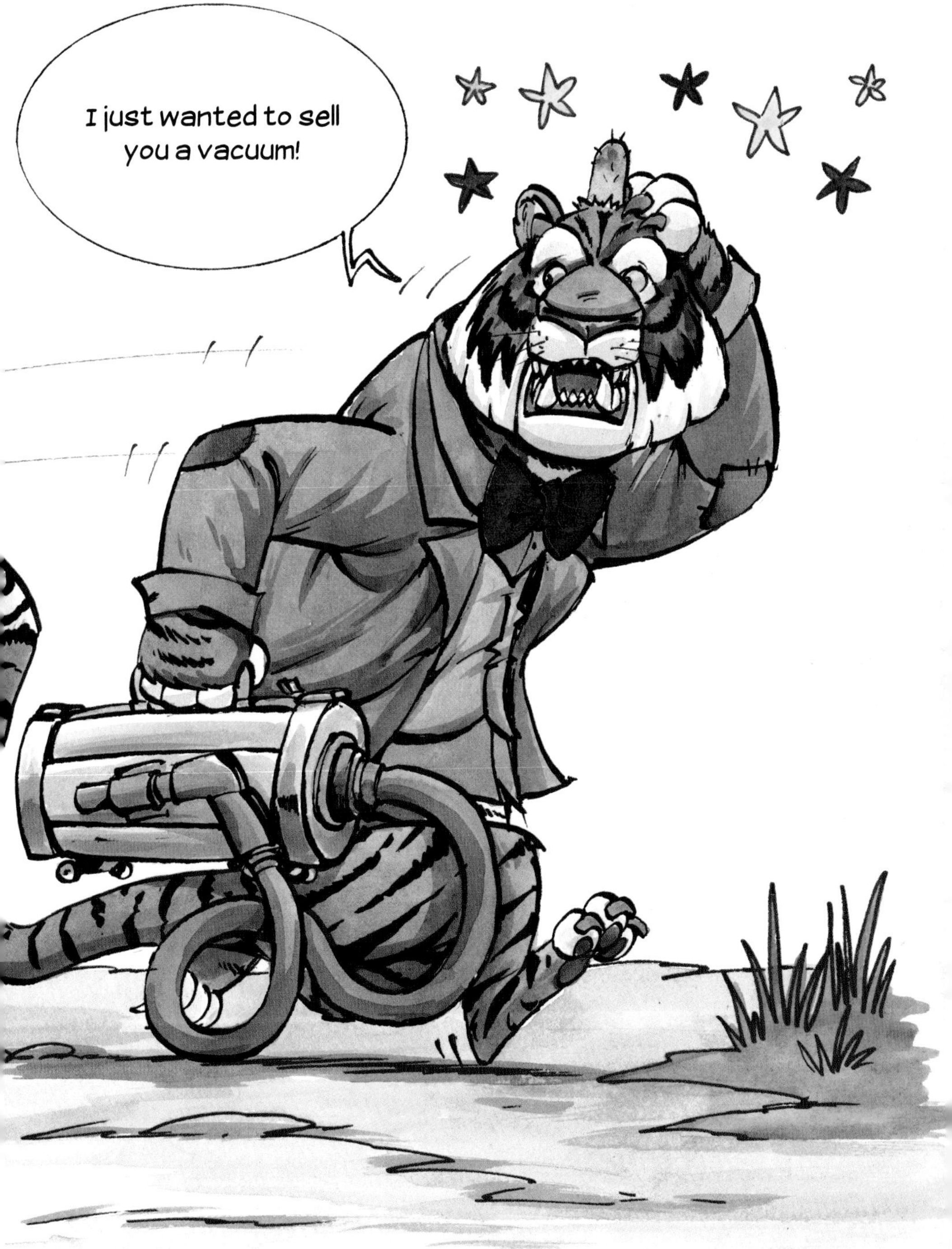
I just wanted to sell you a vacuum!

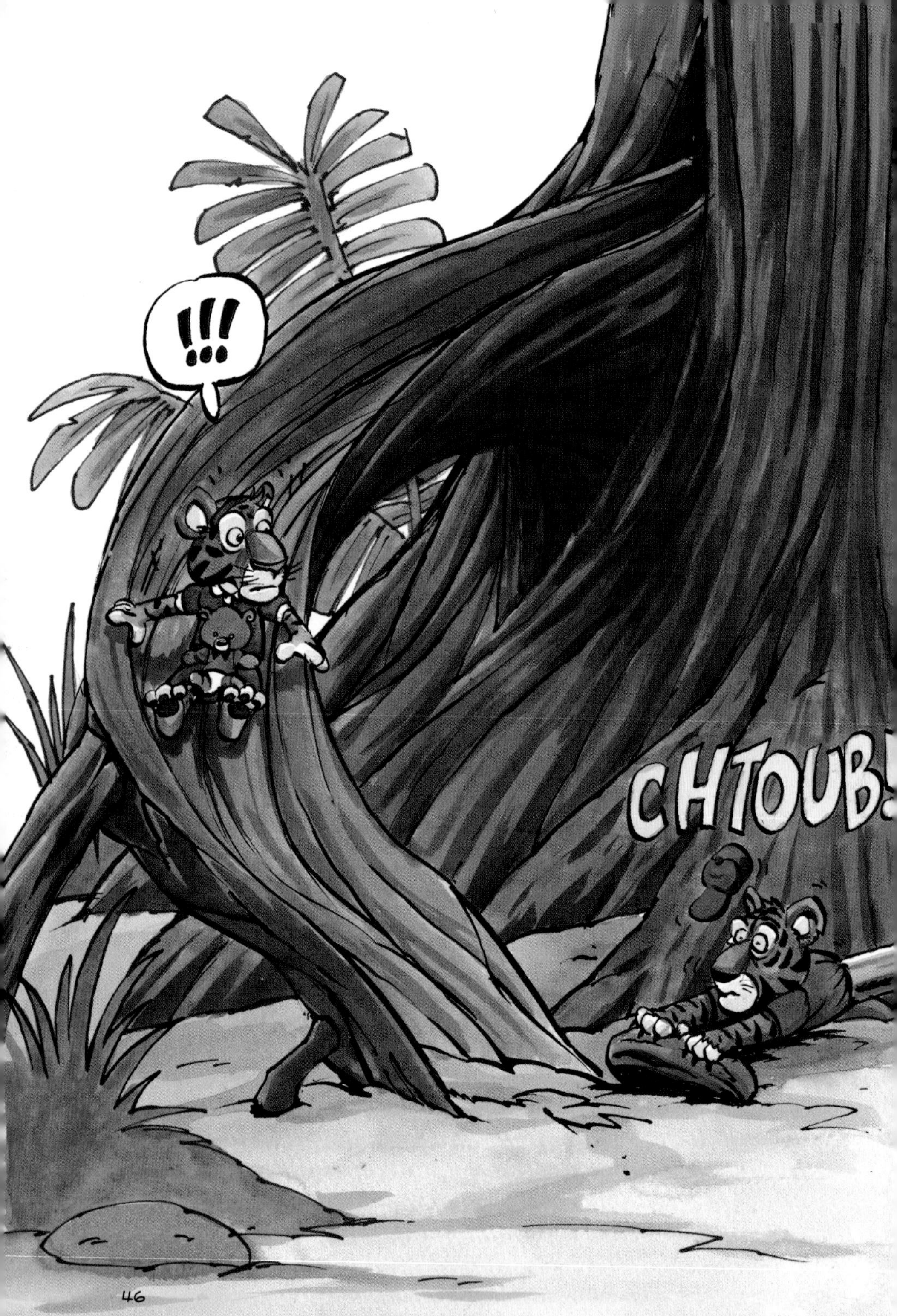
!!!
CHTOUB!

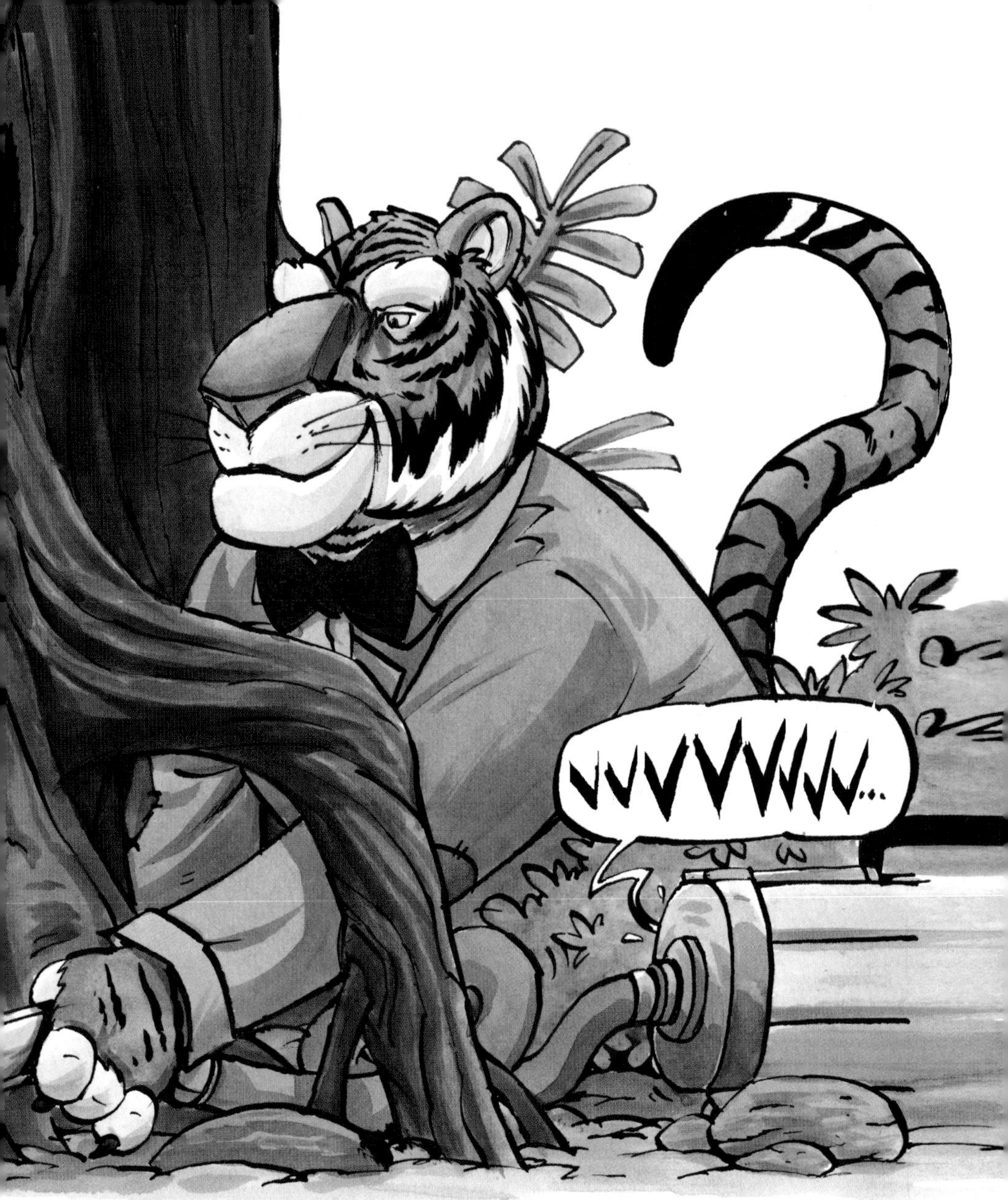
VVVVVVVV...

Infanticide is the number one cause of death in tigers under one year of age.

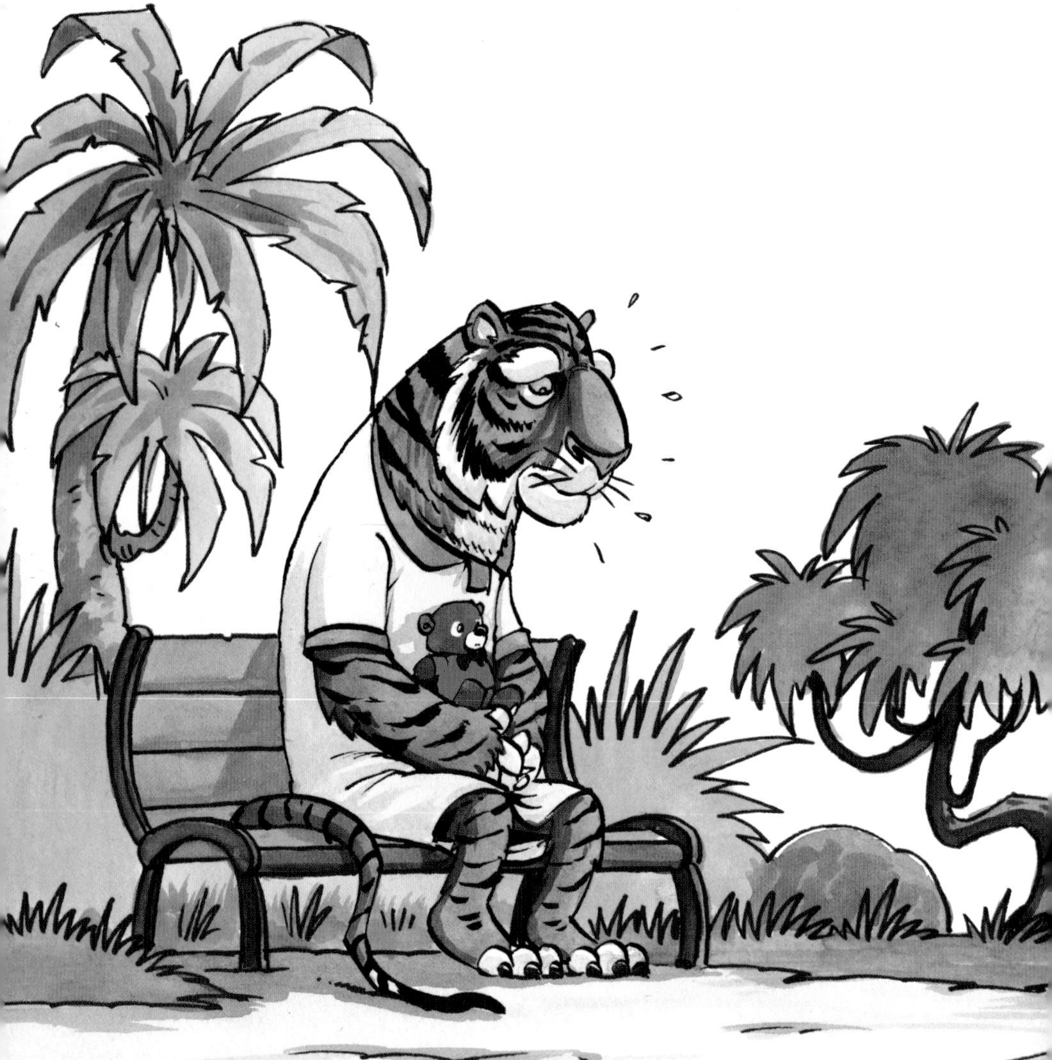

Once the male tiger kills the cubs, the female comes into **heat** again and the male can then generate his own offspring.

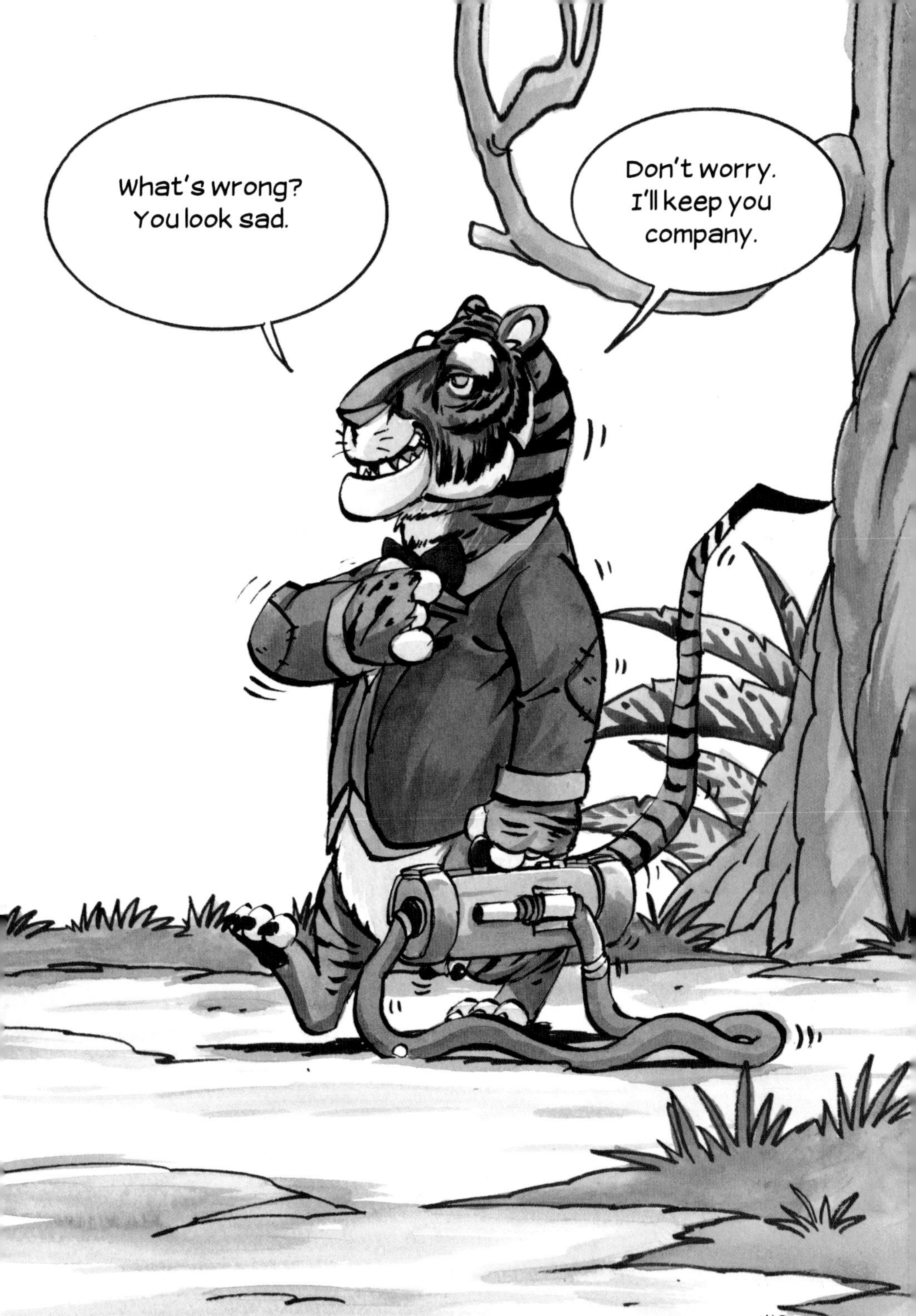
What's wrong?
You look sad.
Don't worry.
I'll keep you
company.

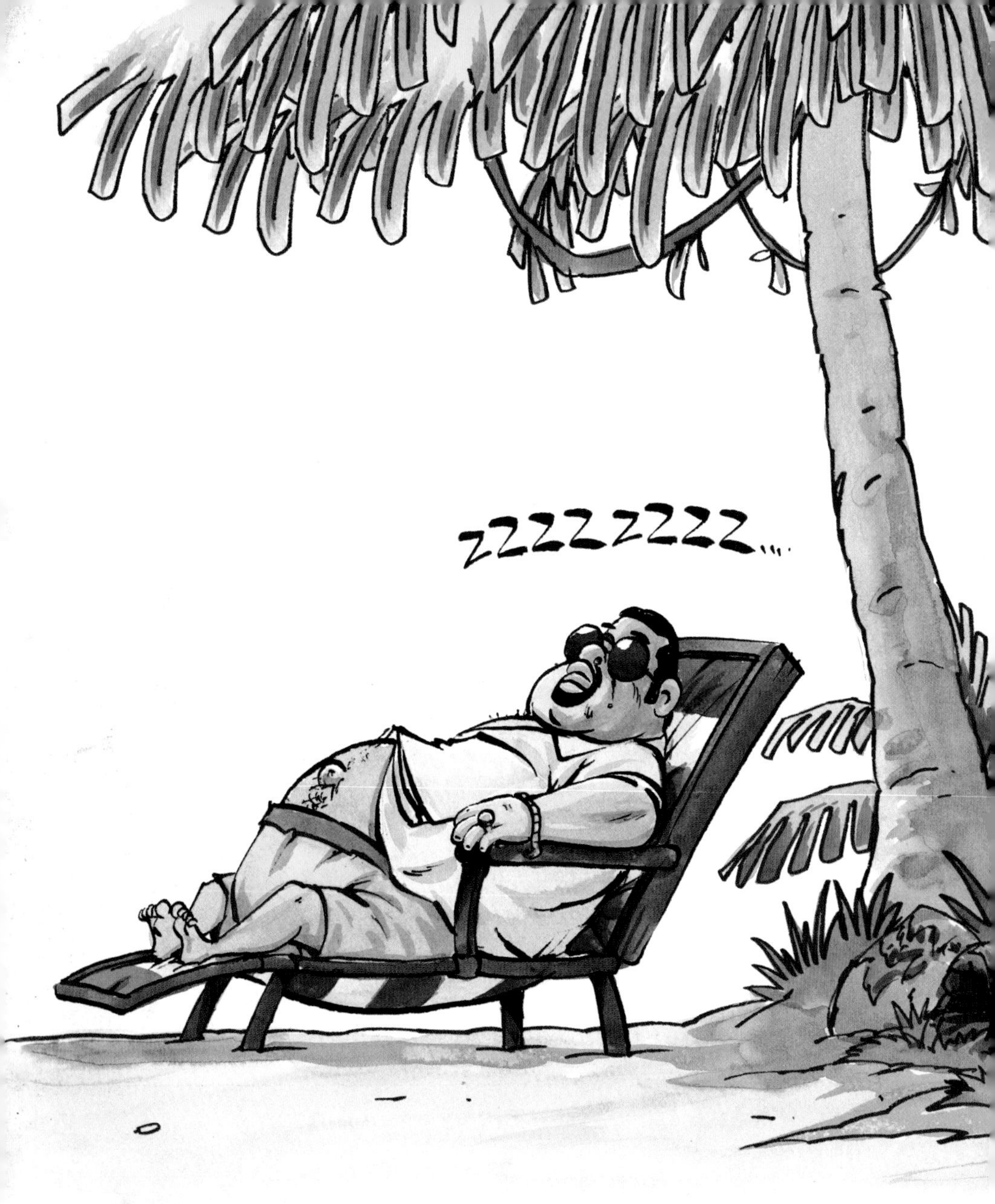
ZZZZZZZZ....

Because they occasionally attack humans, lions have been deemed "man eaters." Tigers, on the other hand, generally avoid having contact with humans. There are approximately 50 to 100

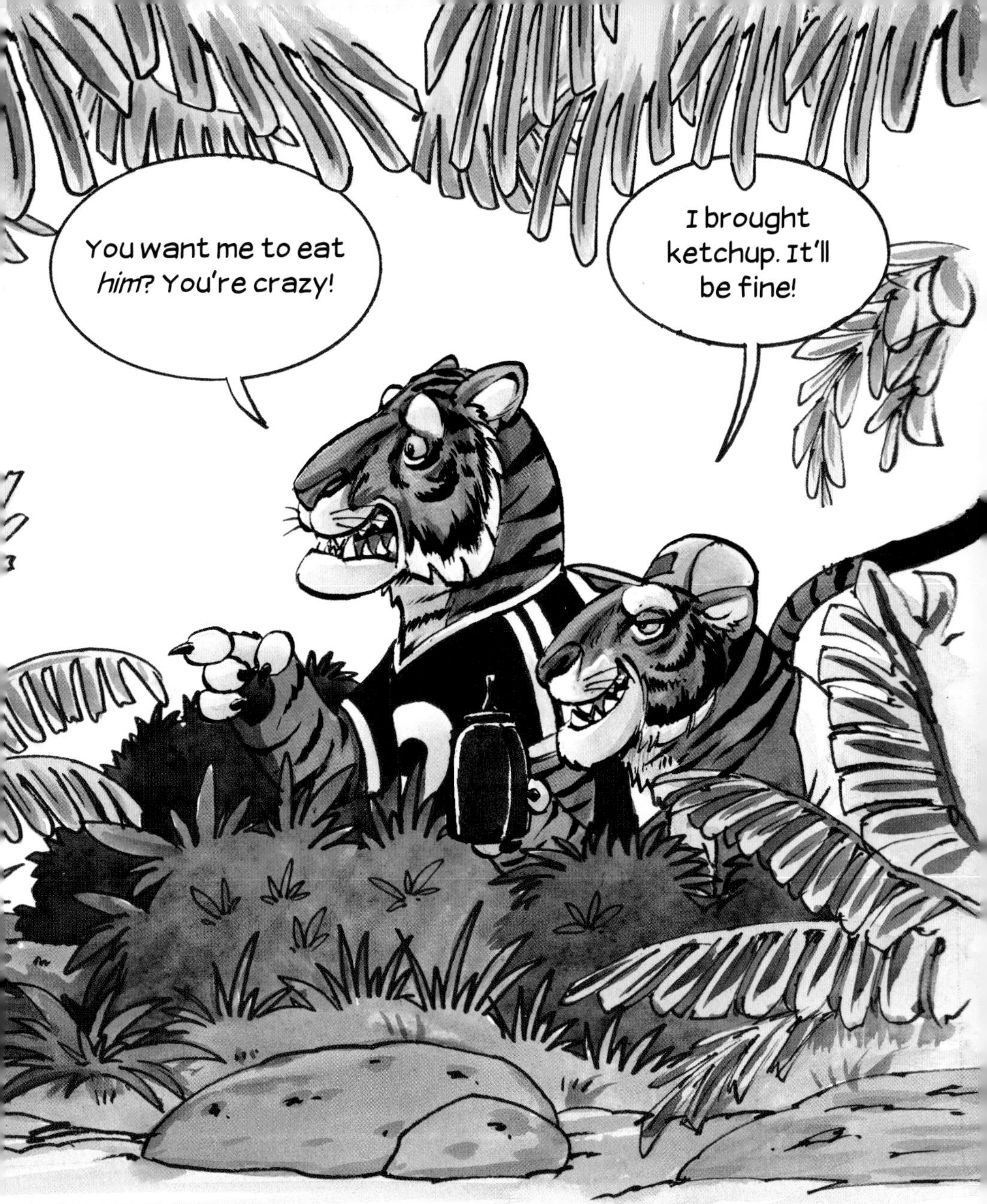
You want me to eat *him*? You're crazy!
I brought ketchup. It'll be fine!

human deaths by tigers around the world each year, mostly in India.

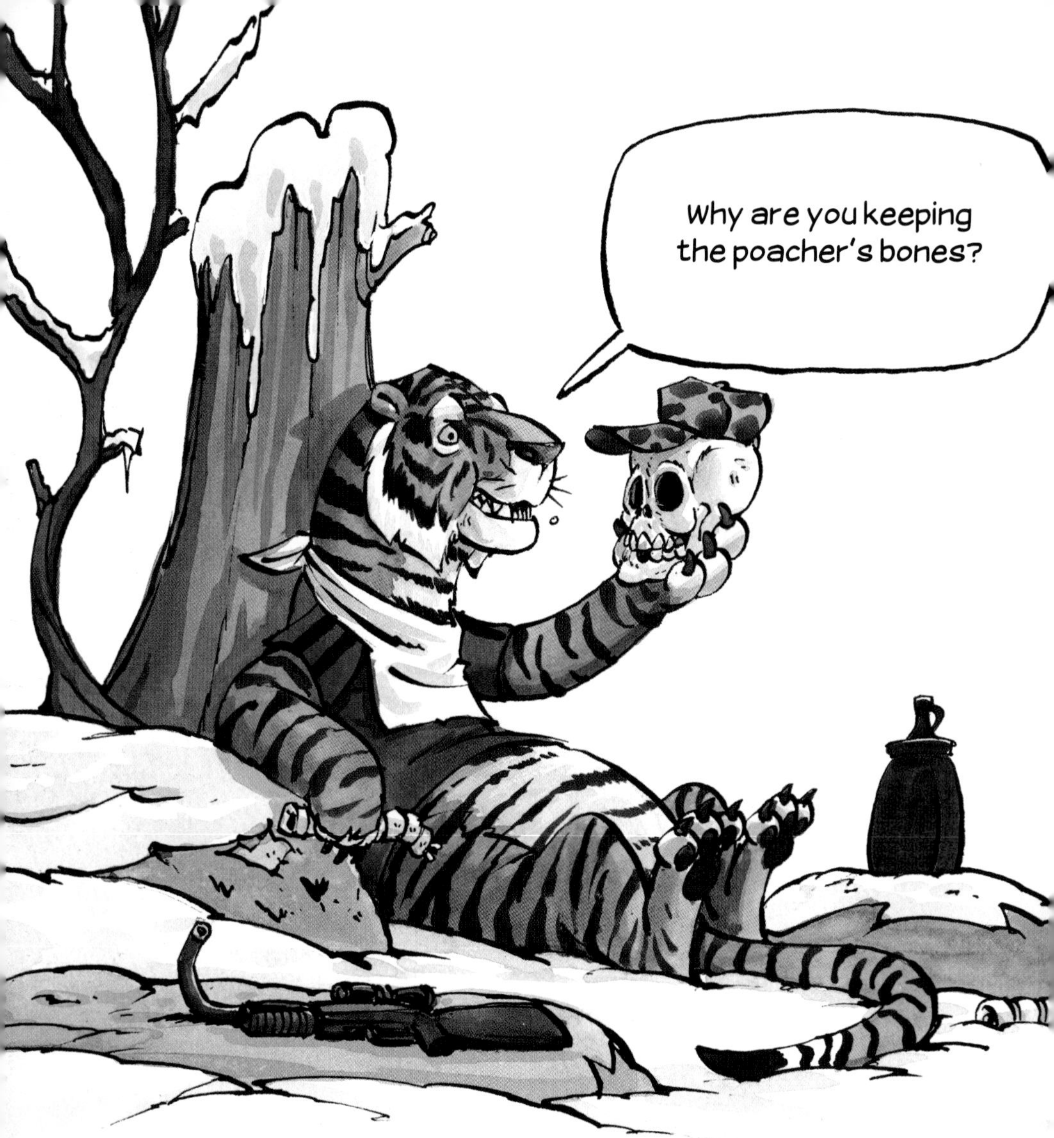
Why are you keeping the poacher's bones?

On the Chinese market, a tiger skeleton can make **poachers** a lot of money. **Traditional Chinese Medicine** often calls for the rare tiger bones.

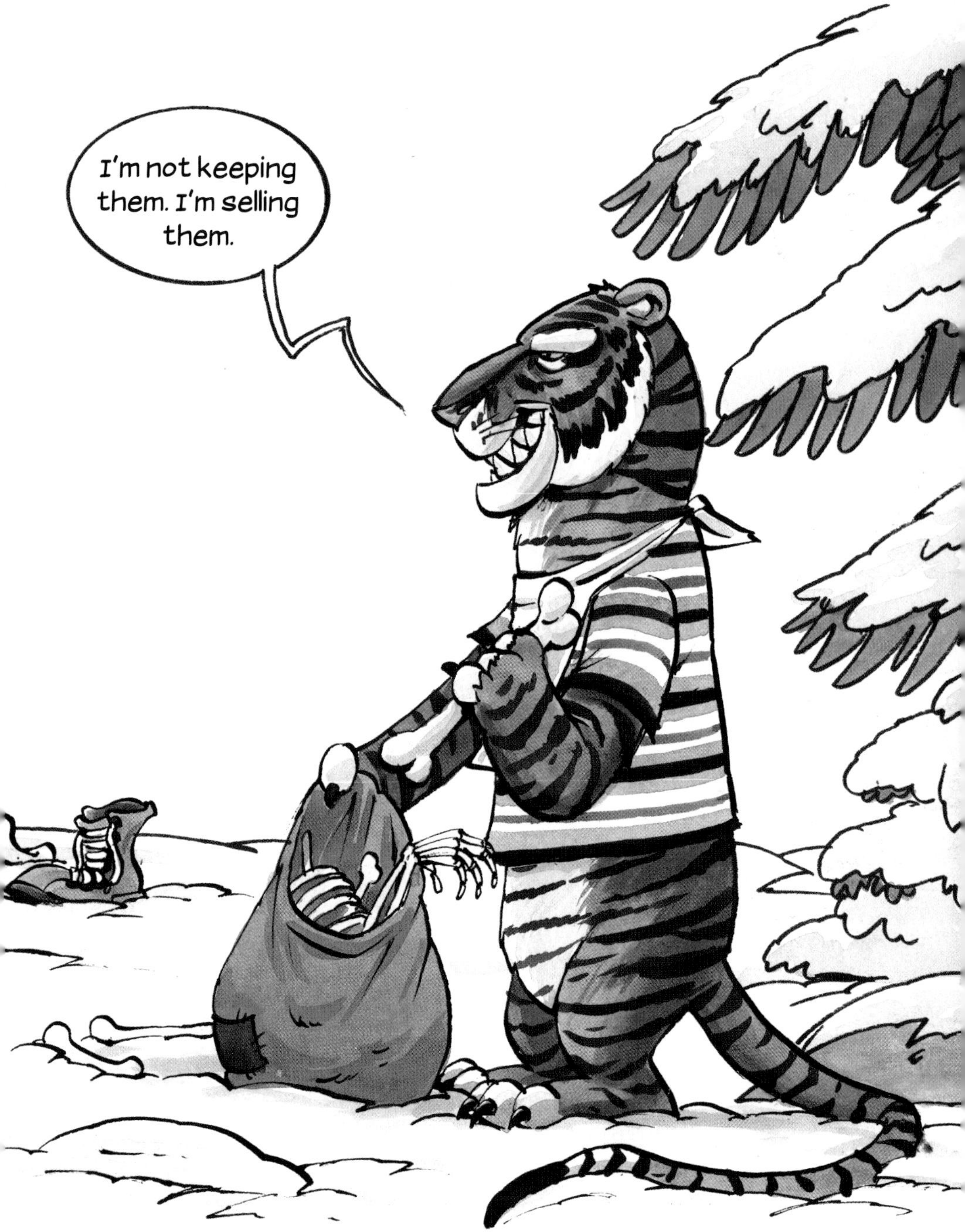
I'm not keeping them. I'm selling them.

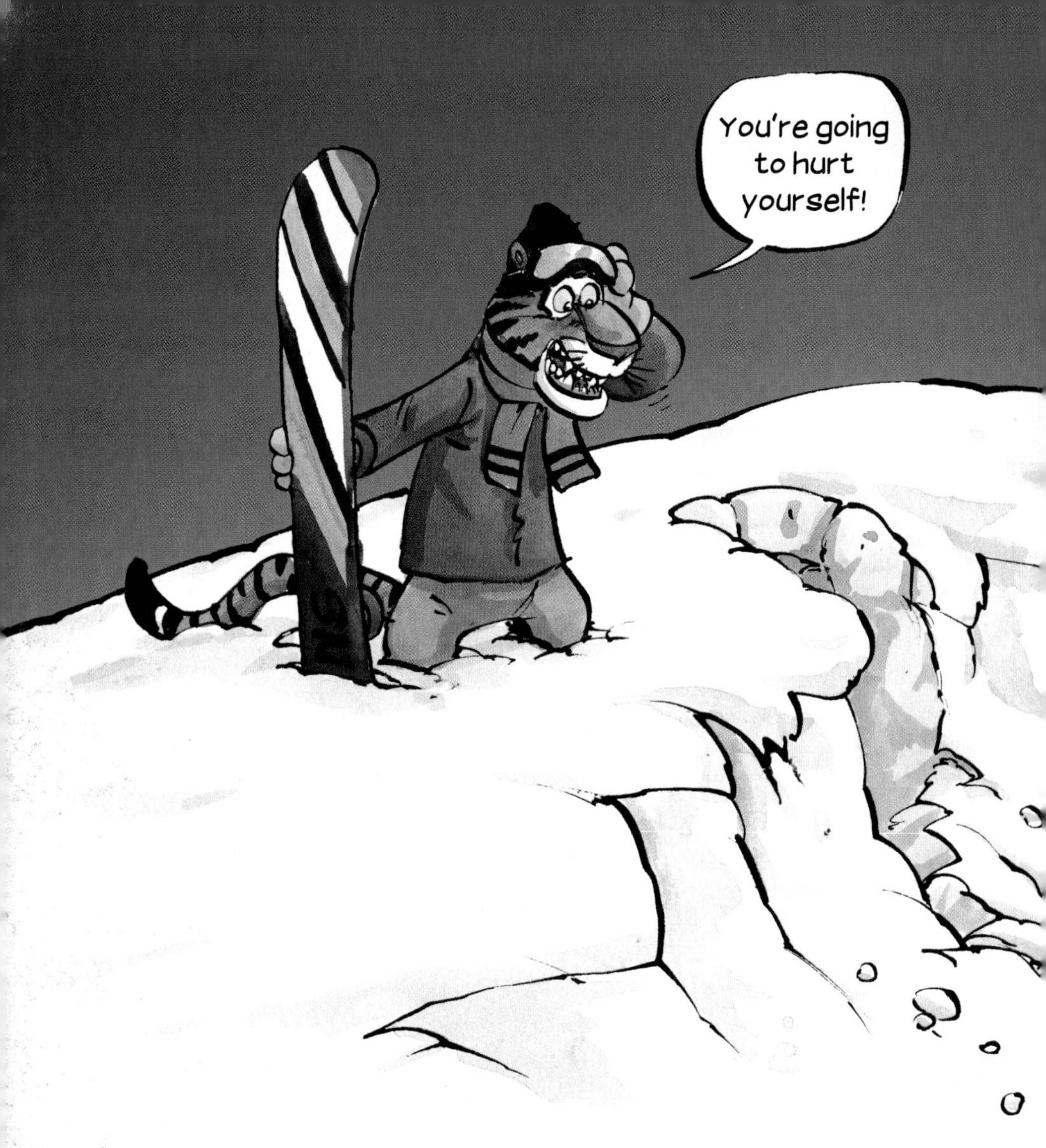
You're going to hurt yourself!

In India, the number of tigers has dropped by half in the past 5 years. There were approximately 40,000 tigers in the year 1915, but there are only approximately 1,000 left today. That's an average of one tiger death per day.

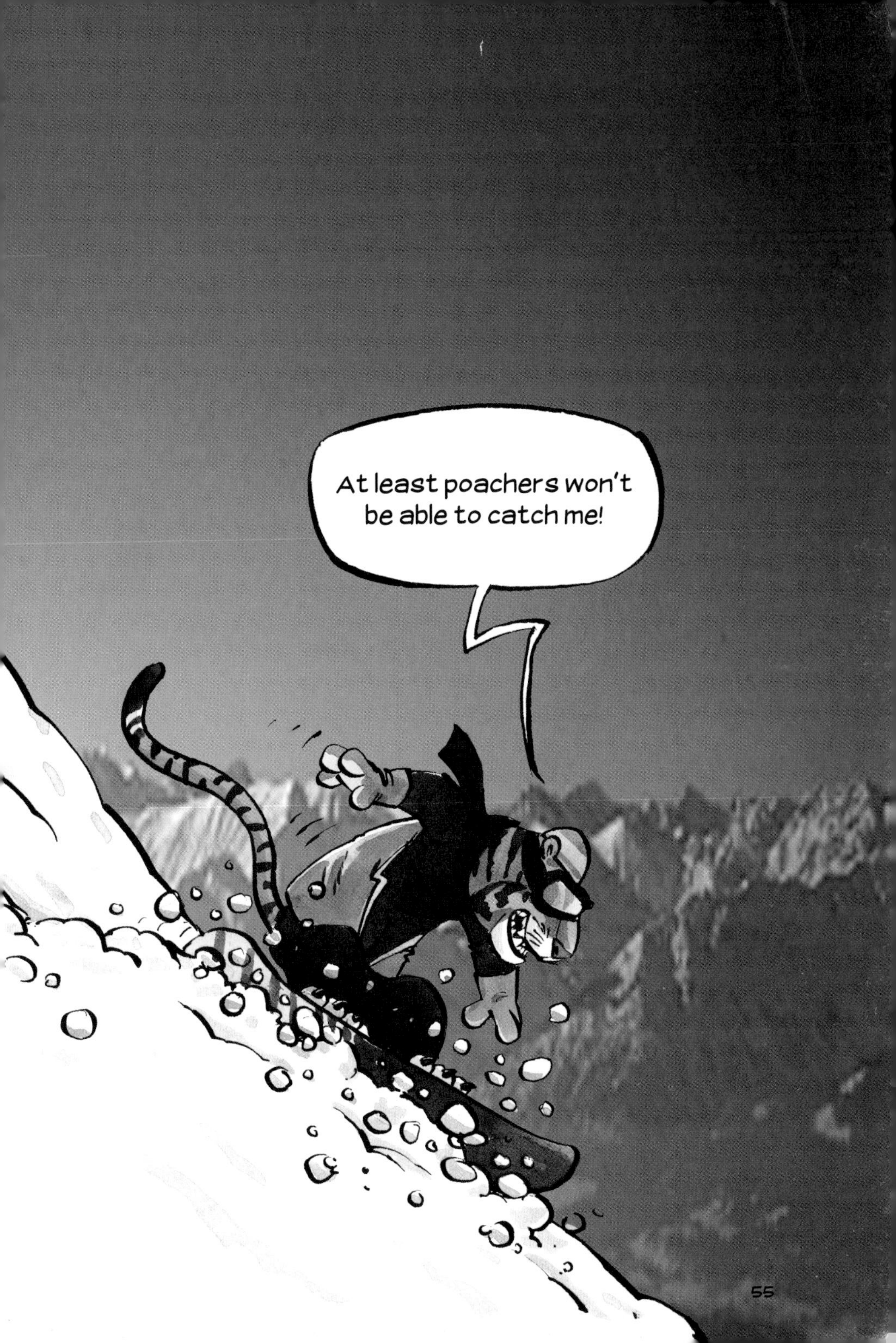
At least poachers won't be able to catch me!

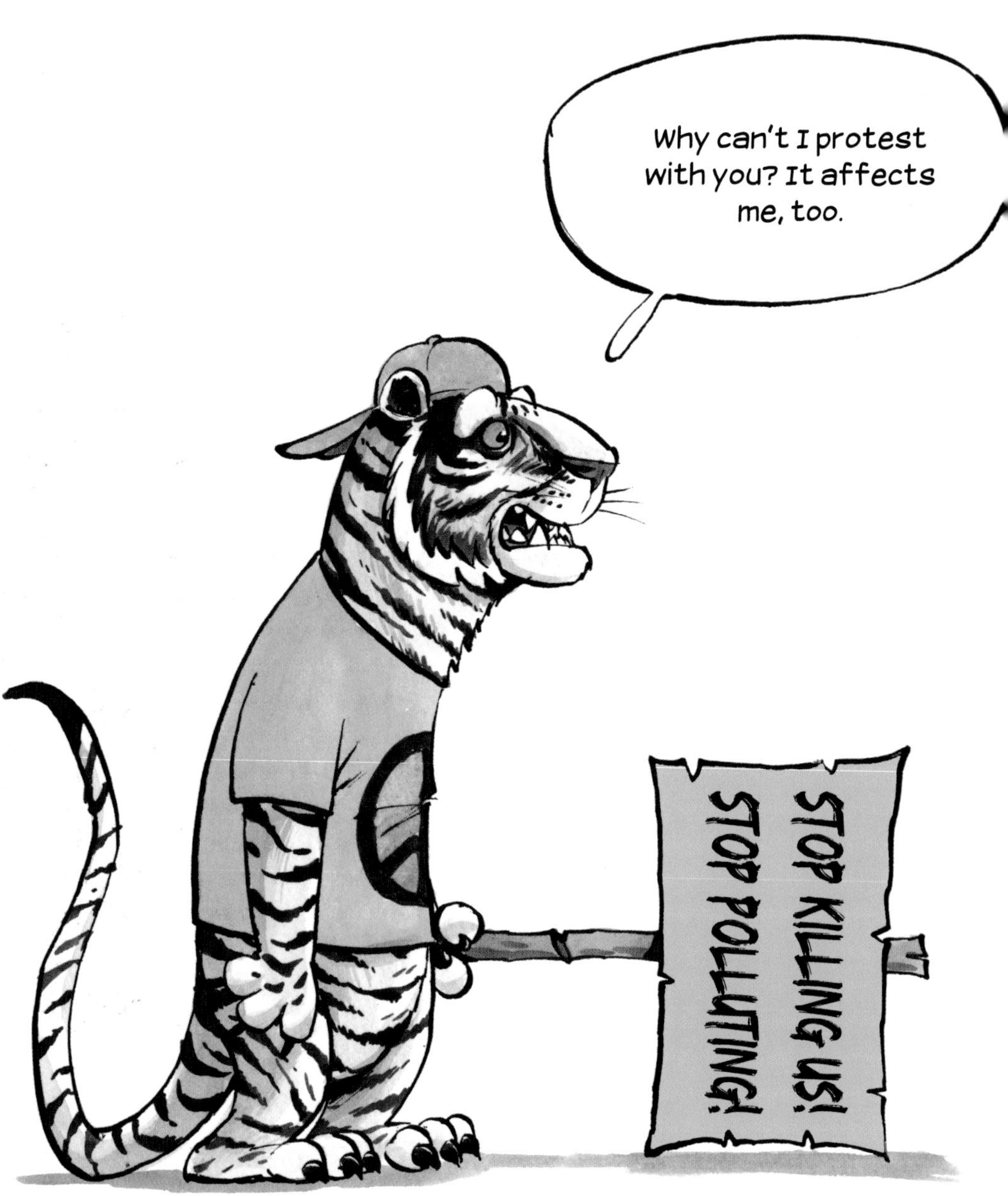
Why can't I protest with you? It affects me, too.
STOP KILLING US!
STOP POLLUTING!

Tigers are an **endangered** species. There are less than 3,500 individuals in the wild. Of the 6 subspecies, 3 have become **extinct** in the past 50 years.

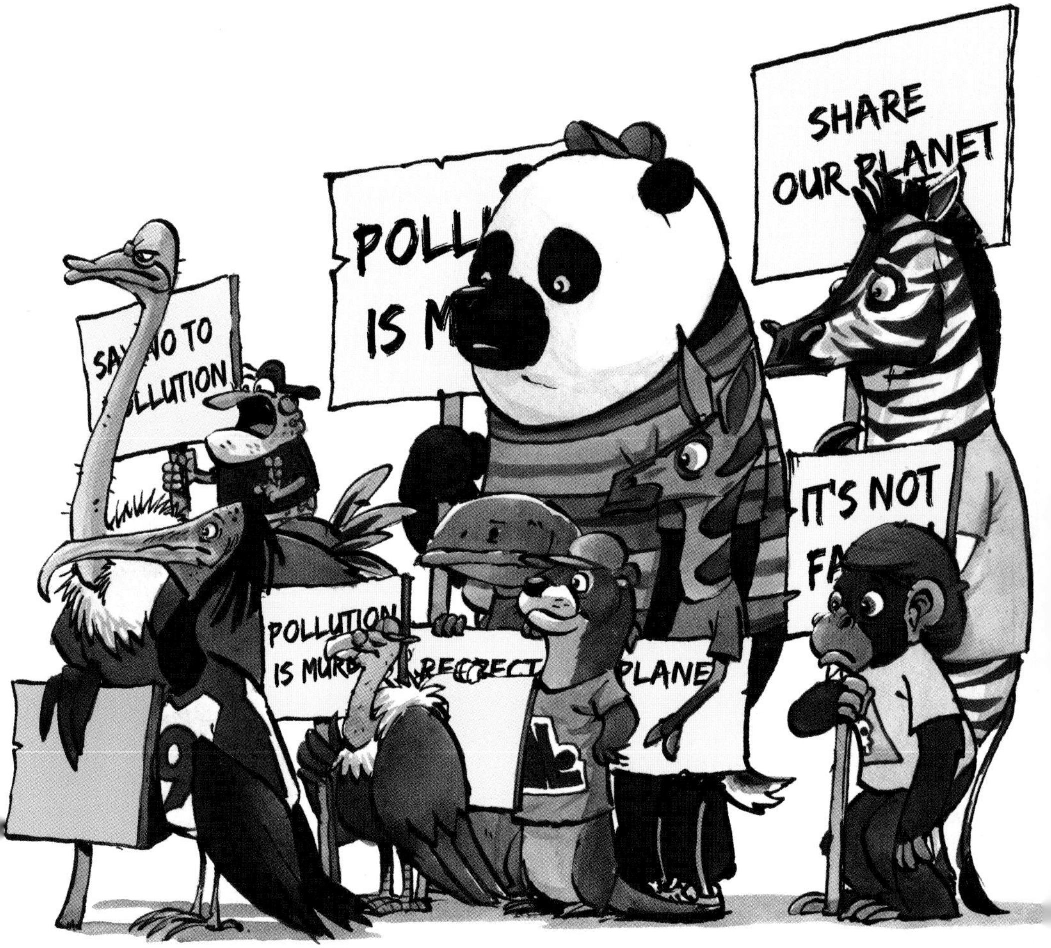
SHARE
OUR PLANET
POLL
IS M
SAY NO TO
LLUTION
IT'S NOT
FA
POLLUTION
IS MURD
PLANE

Glossary

Carnivore a meat-eater

Endangered threatened with extinction

Extinct a species of plant or animal that has died out completely

Feline a member of the cat family

Heat when a female is ready to mate

Infanticide the act of killing a baby

Mammal a warm-blooded, back-boned animal

Poacher a person who hunts or catches animals illegally

Prey an animal hunted and killed by another for food

Solitary living alone

Species a classification of a group of creatures with common characteristics

Subspecies a division of a species into smaller groups with common characteristics

Terrestrial living on land

Traditional Chinese Medicine an ancient healthcare system based on Chinese traditions

Index

Do You Know there are other titles?

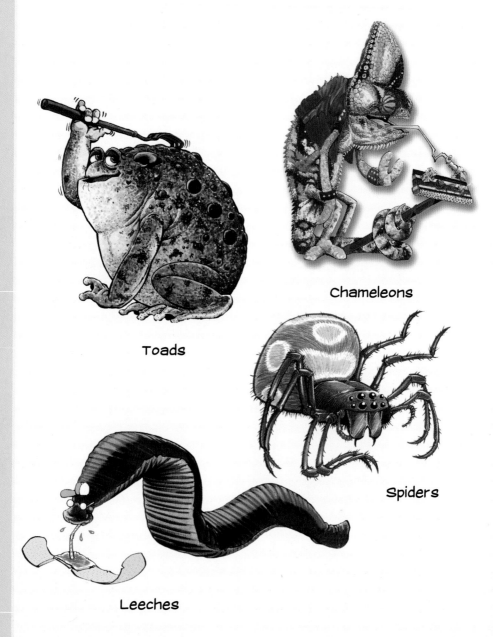

Chameleons

Toads

Spiders

Leeches

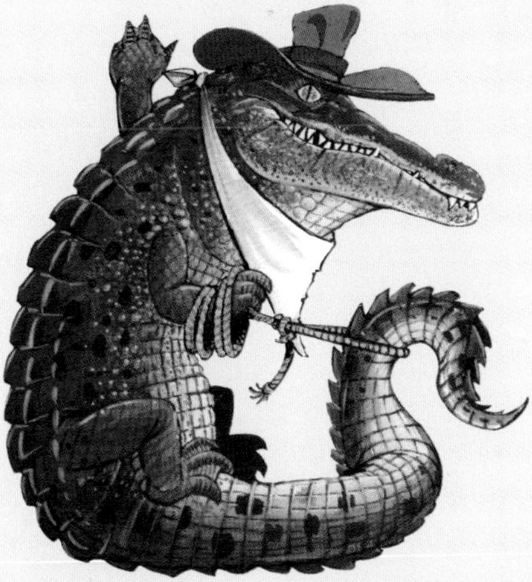

Crocodiles

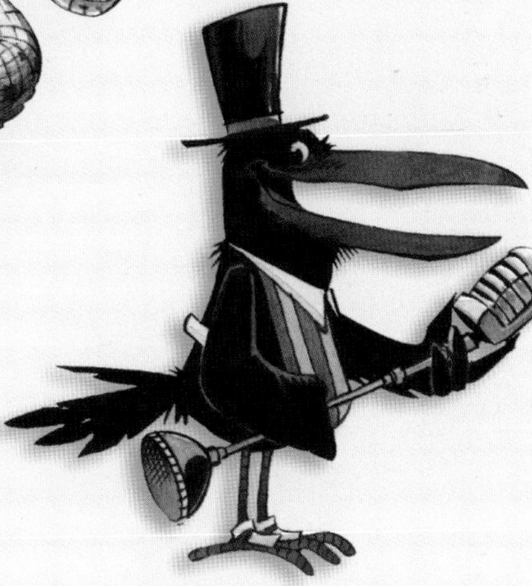

Crows

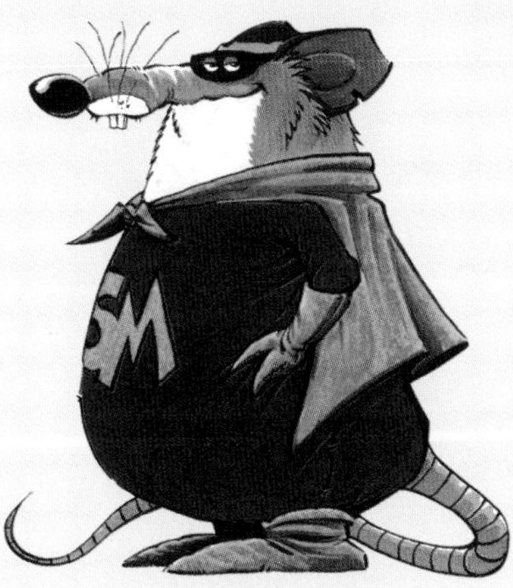
SM

Rats

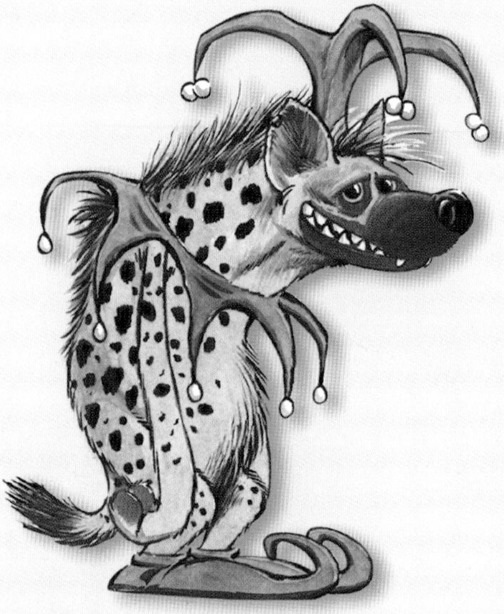

Hyenas

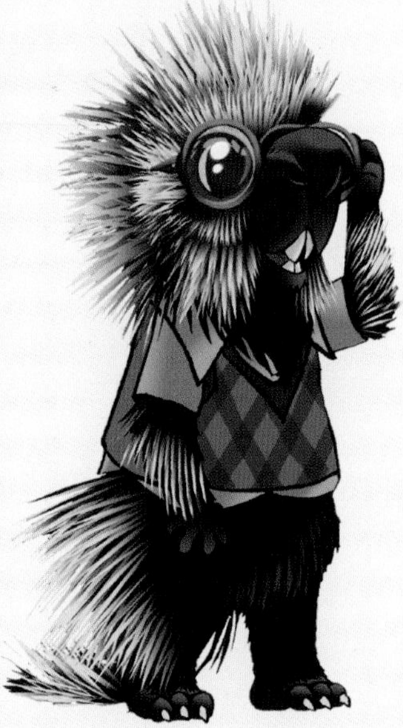

Porcupines

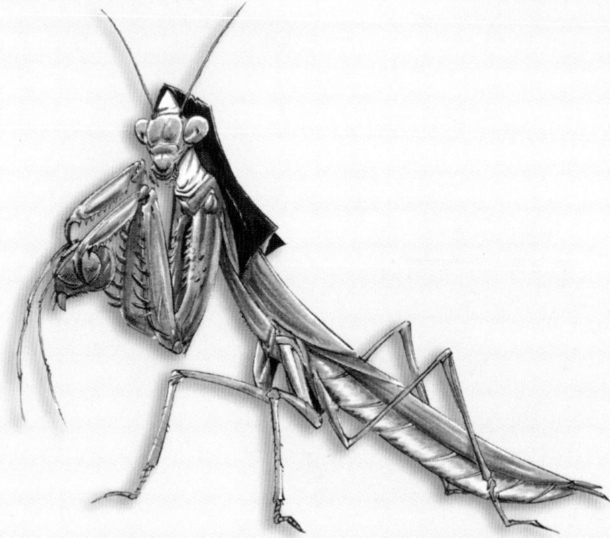

Praying Mantises

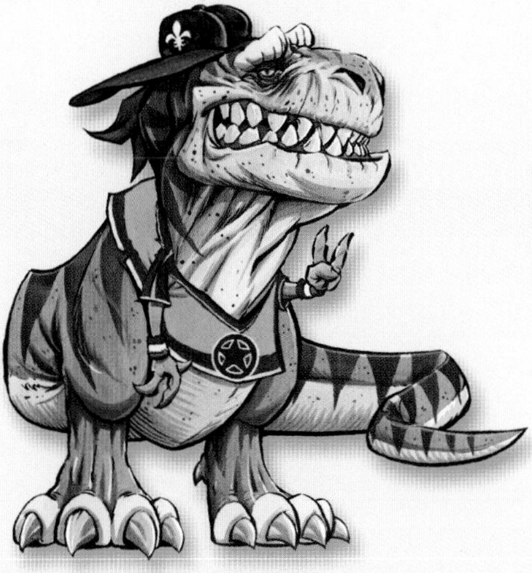

Dinosaurs

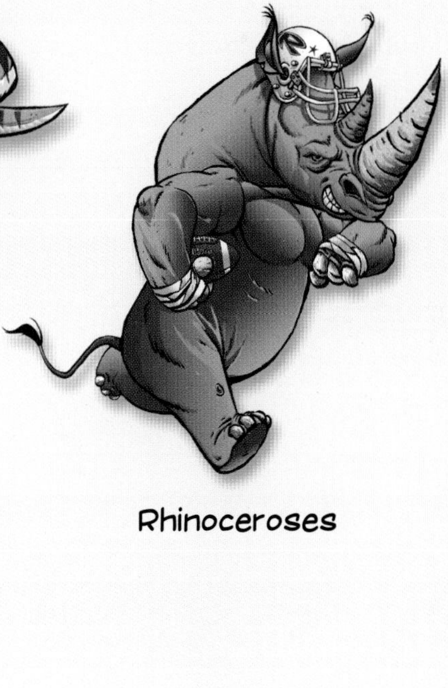

Rhinoceroses

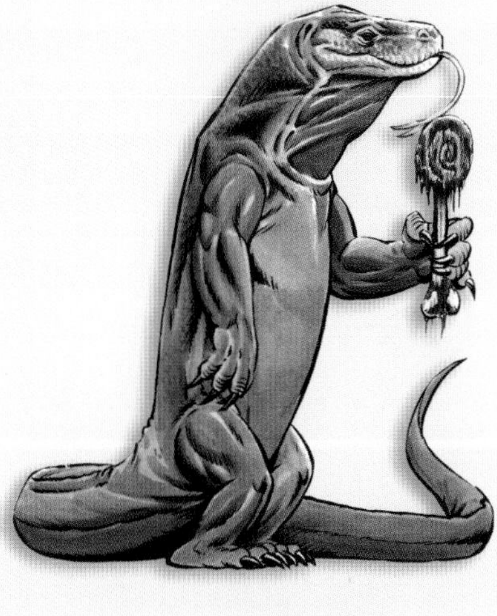

Komodo Dragons